LIVING BA

LIVING BAPTISM

CALLED OUT OF THE ORDINARY

CLARE WATKINS

DARTON·LONGMAN+TODD

First published in 2006 by
Darton, Longman and Todd Ltd
1 Spencer Court
140—142 Wandsworth High Street
London
SW18 4JJ

ISBN 0 232 52662 1

A catalogue record for this book is available from
the British Library.

Printed and bound in Great Britain by
The Cromwell Press, Trowbridge, Wiltshire

With
my husband Guy
for
our children
Christopher, Michael, Alice and Stephen

CONTENTS

INTRODUCTION

Let us be clear, right at the start, what this book is about, and what it is *not* about. The title tells us, unequivocally, that our subject is *baptism*. But, if this is a book about baptism, it is, just as much, a book about *living*. In particular, it is about living as a baptised person in today's world, in ways which consistently recall and live out what it means to be baptised. It is about practically embodying baptism in our everyday lives.

Baptism is not a simple matter, and nor is its living out in ordinary lives. These ideas make demands upon us, and will not always be immediately accessible, or comfortable. After all, we are talking about Christian discipleship, with reference to our own rather muddled-up lives. But if these are not simple, straightforward matters, they are, just the same, matters of vitality and importance in the lives of men and women, whatever the situation we find ourselves in concerning baptism itself.

For there is not one, single experience of baptism to be addressed here. For some of us, our own baptisms may be a long-distant event, one which we rarely think of, even something 'done to us' without our knowledge or consent, if we were baptised as infants. We may be glad of it, resent it, or be indifferent to it. For others, baptism may be a celebration fresh in their memory; for others again, baptism lies ahead as something yet to be celebrated, and still to be thought about and decided on. It may be, too, that a person's most pressing sense of baptism is focused on the decision to have their child baptised or not. If you fall into any of these categories, this book is addressed to you. In it, the idea of 'living baptism' is offered as a help in deepening our understanding of how the simple, common ritual of baptism has the potential to transform our living into something more joyous, more truth-full, more fully human – more of God, in fact.

In all this variety of the experience of baptism, we are confronted with the central concern of this book: that is, the way in which baptism is *both* a ritual, church service, or celebration, *and*, at the same time, says something bigger about our lives, where we belong, how we see the world, and where we're headed. Baptism presents itself most obviously as a simple human act; but it is also, in all its language, significance and symbolism, an opening up of mystery – the mystery of God, revealed in Jesus.

There are rather a lot of books on baptism for the 'church professional' – ministers, priests, theologians. Such books are often most concerned with questions of baptismal policy, and liturgical or sacramental practice and validity. For very good reasons the 'professional' end of the thinking around baptism has been caught up with questions of *who* should be baptised, whether one might re-baptise, how does baptism need to be performed in order to be, properly, baptism. These are important and serious questions, and they are not irrelevant to what follows here. Still, they seem, too often, to be in danger of missing the point. What, after all, *is* 'the point' of baptism, for the ordinary person, living day to day in an un-churchy and often post-Christian environment?

The questions that arise from this ordinary place of Christian living are different from the professionals' questions:

- What difference (if any) has baptism made, or might it make, to my ordinary, 'secular' life?
- How, if I am already baptised, do I respond, day by day, to my baptism?
- What do I do (if anything) on a daily basis, to nurture the baptism of others – my children, my spouse, my baptised friends (whether 'actively Christian' or not)?

These are questions central to the mystery of baptism; they sum up the need for an understanding of *living baptism*. For the real mystery of this sacrament is in its ordinary living, day by day, of the extraordinariness of life in Jesus Christ, which is now and yet to come.

This is the way this book seeks to rediscover baptism: going out from the ceremonies, and courses, and policies, and finding a fresh and living *theology*, baptism's spiritual reality, in the living of baptismal mystery 'in ordinary'.

To serve this purpose, the major part of this book is given over to chapters which first reflect on an aspect of the mystery of baptism, and then follow through this presentation of the Christian tradition with an exploration of what difference it all makes to human living. The first three chapters (Part 1) are more general. They look at the theology of baptism beyond the ritual experience and practice (Chapter 1) and its implications for our understanding of Church and of the Christian life today (Chapter 2). What becomes clear is that the long theological tradition surrounding baptism presents us with a rich, multi-denominational source for a living of baptism as something transformative of the everyday (Chapter 3).

Part 2 (Chapters 4–8) looks in more depth at five traditions in baptismal theology and ritual. In each chapter, the scriptural witness to, and rituals of, baptism lead into an exploration of a part of the Christian faith proclaimed in baptism (*'Exploring the tradition'*). After this presentation of something of the Christian theological tradition, some more practical, everyday suggestions are made as to how this tradition might change things for our day-to-day living (*'Living the mystery'*). The central conviction is that we cannot really speak fully about baptism, unless we speak at the same time about living our lives – here and now, and towards God.

Finally, the Epilogue offers a reflection on baptismal living as the call to live God's own life in the world.

The remarkable realisation for me, having finished the writing, is that, in the end, the exploration of baptism and its liveable (and loveable!) theology, is nothing less than an exploration of the Christian faith – its wisdom, traditions, beauty and practicality. And the terrain of this exploration is as much to do with everyday living as it is with high theology or distant spiritualities (though all these things are needed together!). It is this life of exploration that baptism invites us into, more and more deeply. It is a blessed adventure!

PART ONE

RESHAPING OUR UNDERSTANDING OF BAPTISM

CHAPTER ONE

BAPTISM AND CHRISTIAN DISCIPLESHIP

> *Go, therefore, and make disciples of all the nations, baptising them ...*
> Matthew 28:19

> *Now when they heard this they were cut to the heart and said to Peter and the other apostles, 'Brothers, what should we do?' Peter said to them, 'Repent, and be baptised every one of you ...'* Acts 2:37–8

Baptism presents itself to most of us in terms of a ritual, or celebration, or liturgy. It is, indeed, such a thing; but the argument of this book is based on the conviction that baptism is, at the same time, something much more than this, something beyond the church service, and something to which the church services point. In this first chapter we will look, a little more, at this conviction, and set out some of the ways in which the celebration of baptism, itself, draws us out to life after the celebration. The ritual, fully understood, compels us into a transformed way of living – a living of baptism.

The two quotes from the New Testament which start this chapter draw our attention to the fundamental nature of baptism as something that Christians from the beginning have *done*. Indeed, as the words from Matthew's Gospel make clear, Jesus' followers are commanded by the risen Lord himself to baptise. In this way – with teaching, we should note (Matt. 28:20) – the apostles make new disciples all over the world. So it is that, in the second quote, after Peter's great preaching at Pentecost, when his hearers are moved to respond, it is baptism, with repentance, that is the thing that gives shape to their response of faith. Peter leads his hearers to belief in Jesus, and they ask what they should do; the answer is, be baptised. Baptism is, simply, one of the things that is done by the Christian community, from the beginning, at that moment of faith, the coming to be of a new disciple.

Baptism can be seen, in this way, as a concrete action, a 'thing done', or a ritual carried out. This is something with which we are familiar. And because it refers us to a concrete 'doing', and action, we find baptism rather easier to focus on than the other commands that surround these verses. The calls to teach, and to repent, are difficult, and abstract in comparison. Baptism, on the other hand, is a particular set of actions and words that take place in a church, at a given time. It is an event.

The danger is that, because of this concrete, do-able nature, baptism appears to us as something we can grasp, use, understand. We can do the deed, and think that everything has been accomplished, whereas teaching and repentance are rather more daunting and open-ended in their doing.

Yet within the very practicality of the event of baptism, we will find a language, of word and symbol, which draws us beyond the event itself, into something altogether bigger, less straightforward, and less graspable. Everything about this action assumes and calls us to repentance, teaching, learning, and growth. It calls us to living, in fact. Indeed, more than this: it tells about *transformed living*, the 'fullness of life', and life with God forever.

THE DOING OF BAPTISM

A brief look at the actual doing of baptism can begin to give some flesh to this last thought. In fact, this is the concern of all that follows, and what we begin with here is just a distant view of the landscape to be journeyed through. To start with, we need to have in mind the ways in which what actually happens in baptism speaks of the sacrament's nature as an event, a done thing, which, all the same, draws those participating into something bigger, deeper, beyond the actions themselves.[1]

So, even the obvious and apparently unremarkable fact that baptism usually takes place in a church, with a gathering of people of some kind, speaks to us of the greater thing that is going on here. Here is no private affair, no simply individual or even family event. This is an event of a community, and, more particularly, of the community of Jesus, which is marked by the sign of the cross. So the signing with the cross, which is a part of the baptismal rite of very many Christians, is also a sign of welcome and belonging, as the one to be baptised is brought into a larger community, and bound to them in the love of God, which shines out from Jesus dying for us:

> ... the Christian community welcomes you with great joy. In its name I claim you for Christ our Saviour by the sign of his cross. I now trace the cross on your forehead, and invite your parents to do the same.[2]

A simple, human action, this gathering, welcome, and signing is pointing us to the profound reality of what it is to become a member of Christ's body, a part of the community of Christians, who all bear the sign of the Lord's cross.[3] In a similar way, each part of what is happening in the church celebration speaks of something mysterious, beyond ourselves. The reading and hearing of Scriptures, which we are called to receive as God's revealing of himself to us, leads into a profession of faith. This profession of faith gives human words to the great mysteries of the Christian faith, and so expresses that strange realisation that, in faith, human beings can speak of God, and know him more deeply.

Central, of course, to the celebration of baptism is the use of water, an absolute fact of baptism from the beginning, and recognised as essential (normally!) by all Christians.[4] This simple and essential element speaks to us of life, of washing, and also – in its natural power – of death. The tradition of fully immersing the one being baptised in water is a vivid reminder of the way in which baptism joins us to Christ's saving death, and so to his new life in the resurrection.[5] There is a sense in which we are drowned by the waters of baptism!

This newness of life in Christ's Easter mystery is also proclaimed symbolically in the ancient tradition of the wearing of the white garment,[6] and in the giving of the lighted candle.[7] Within the Catholic tradition this light given to the newly baptised is lit from the Paschal (Easter) candle, making clearer still the connection between the radiance of this new Christian life and the glory of the Lord's resurrection.

These are simply a few examples of how the ordinary-looking actions of the ritual of baptism speak of things beyond themselves

– beyond, in fact, all our best imaginings; for how can we imagine that transcendent reality of resurrected life in God of which baptism speaks? These acts, and more – anointing with oil, the Trinitarian formula, the invocation of the Holy Spirit – will be the foundations of our thinking in what follows. For now, what is important is to recognise how the ordinary and extraordinary, the human doing and the divine mystery, come together in this celebration of baptism. Such coming together compels us into ever new ways of living our human lives, in God's grace and promise.

BAPTISM AS THE 'THING DONE' – AND THE DONE THING?

In the light of all this, we can begin to see more clearly the connection between baptism and living. When we turn to look at baptism as 'a Christian doing', we are fixing our gaze on one of those places in Christian life which makes unusual demands of us – if we let it. From wherever we are – as 'active' church members, lay people or clergy, or as people somehow on the margins of church, or as people of no Christian commitment – wherever it is we find ourselves, to look, even briefly, at the event of baptism is to involve our thinking in a distinctive and rather curious activity. For in baptism the routine and practical meets the mysterious and mystical. Here is a place, typical of Christian sacrament, where men and women 'do things' with very ordinary stuff like water, or bread, or oil, and use quite extraordinary language to speak of what *God himself* is doing there. To say that, with this washing in water this person is saved, freed from sin, or that this dripping of oil onto their heads makes them part of God's Kingdom of priests – well, it is rather an odd juxtaposition of the mundane and the divine.

It is, perhaps, reassuring to discover that this sense of the oddness of baptism is not peculiar to the contemporary mind. People have always found it frankly strange, if not downright silly. In fact, such 'silliness' is entirely proper to Christian sacrament and life. Tertullian, way back in the second century, was as aware as anyone today how strange a claim it is to say that in baptismal washing we are saved from sin:

> There is absolutely nothing which makes men's minds more obdurate than the simplicity of the divine works which are visible in the act [the doing], when compared with the grandeur which is thereby promised in the effect [what we proclaim is really going on]. So that from the very fact, that with so great simplicity, without pomp, without any considerable novelty of preparation, finally without expense, a man is dipped in water, and amid the utterance of some few words, is sprinkled, and then rises again, not much (or not at all) the cleaner, the consequent attainment of eternity is esteemed the more incredible.[8]

This is a simple, concrete action, using the most at hand and necessary materials. This is attainment of eternal life. This is baptism.

The big question is how we respond to this oddity. We can dismiss it as just plain silly, or we can overcomplicate it in order to make it appear more sensible. Or we can be left feeling alternately mystified, and resignedly baffled. It is, if we bother to think of it at all, more than a little troubling. In the end, it cries out for *faith*; but even this does not make the trouble go away.

Of course, one very normal response is the pragmatic one that I suppose is most common in our Christian communities. Baptism is a thing Christians do, and have always done; it's very difficult to understand all that is proclaimed in this doing, but we can just get on and do it. In this way baptism moves from being a thing done, to the done thing.

This presents a new set of problems. Such simple pragmatism – just getting on and doing – has its own powerful eloquence, and its own silent betrayals. We need to keep the doing of the ritual always in touch with the bigger mystery it proclaims and makes real, if it is not to become a hollow, or badly misunderstood, act. The danger is that, if we don't think about this 'doing' and about what it is saying to the world, and to our own hearts, then we will get ourselves in some fearful muddles, and end up by proclaiming by our *wrong* doing something we never intended at all. Looking at baptism requires us to begin by looking at our real experience and practice of the doing of this ritual, whilst at the same time looking *through* the rituals and policies and programmes to some deeper, more mysterious reality. Only in this way can we become ever truer to the mysterious-practical, extraordinary-ordinary reality which is Christian baptism.

The experience of baptism – its practical doing – is, of course, varied. It differs from Christian community to Christian community, and takes up slightly different forms even within the same church. To illustrate this a little more clearly, what follows is a description of three real-life experiences of baptising, which can help give a concrete focus to what has been said in this chapter so far. In each case it can be seen how the real mystery of baptism can be both obscured, and expressed, and how thoughtful reflection on the doings themselves can deepen our sense of the claim baptism has on us.

EXPERIENCING BAPTISM

In our own contemporary culture, which might be typified as 'post-Christian' in many ways, the majority of people who are baptised Christians will have been baptised as infants; this is a doing of which we have no memory for ourselves. This means that the experience of baptism which we most commonly have and think about, is the baptism of another – a member of our family, or church, or group of friends. In what follows three different events of baptism are described, based on real experiences. In each case, the basic elements of the ceremony are the same; and, theologically, with the eyes of faith, what happens in each case is the same. Remembering this is important! Each story describes a person becoming a new disciple; but each of these people is in a rather different place from the other. Looking at these similarities and differences, without judgement of people's intentions or good faith, and without wishing to set one practice against another, we can identify some questions that arise. In particular, we can ask about the ways in which the actions of the baptisms speak into a living of discipleship – or not.

STORY 1: A BAPTISM OF 'ALLELUIA!'S

As the usual weekly celebration of the Eucharist begins, the church is, perhaps, a little more packed than usual. There is a quiet, joyful sense of excitement, and a family, who are there in the congregation every week, take up a place at the front, away from their regular place. The Paschal candle is lit, and the opening music is bright and full of the joy of the recent celebration of Easter. Everyone gathered is especially glad, because, as they have all known for some weeks now, today is the Sunday on which the Joneses' new baby, Freddie, is to be baptised and joined to them in a new and deep way in the life of Easter.

The service goes along as usual, until the place after the celebration of the Word of Scripture, when this brand-new person is anointed, prayed for, and baptised with water in the font. He is held aloft – somewhat startled! – and carried down the church, a tiny, perplexed new Christian. The whole congregation sings a series of 'Alleluia!'s, and smiles are unavoidable – as are tears for some.

Afterwards, everyone present is called to remember our own baptisms, and to proclaim our baptismal faith in the ancient credal formula. As we do this, we are each reminded that we, too, are baptised into new life. We contemplate the flame of the Easter candle, lit at baptism, to be kept burning in our own lives. Each one is, in their own way, 'held aloft', and knows himself or herself as a startled, perplexed, renewed Christian.

Freddie, the new Christian, anointed priest, prophet and king, sleeps and burps quietly through the continuing celebration of Eucharist. He is carried to the altar as his parents receive the sacrament, and is blessed, as are all the smallest children, in anticipation of their receiving the Eucharist themselves.

At the end of the familiar service, the blessing is given, and everyone is sent out to spread the Gospel. The Jones family, with Freddie and his sister, are gathered around with smiles and congratulations and assurances of prayer, and small gifts. Other families, the elderly, the younger single people – all are looking forward to seeing him grow week by week.

STORY 2: A BAPTISM OF NIGGLES AND QUESTIONS

The Sunday celebration of the Eucharist has just finished. Friends are catching up with one another, listening to each other's concerns, laughing, grumbling, and restraining children. Near the front of the church, others are praying quietly, deepening the moments following their reception of the sacrament, or reflecting on the Word of Scripture they have heard proclaimed that morning. People come and go, some noisy, some quiet, some busy about the bits and pieces of church organisation. The usual thing.

What is less usual is that, pushing uneasily in at the door is a crowd of remarkably well-dressed (if uncomfortable-looking) men and be-hatted, elegant women. Nobody in the church seems to recognise them. There is a sense of uncertainty among them – are they in the right place? Where should they sit? A group stand edgily smoking in the back porch. It becomes clear that these visitors are here for a baptism. Efforts are made to welcome them. One woman asks who is to be baptised. The name is unknown to the people there – 'Oh, well, you wouldn't know it. We don't really go to church.'

A few of the 'regulars' are asked by the minister to stay, to support with some singing and with prayer, and a number do. And just as well, really. As the celebrating crowd gather, the chatter and the exclamations of greeting become overwhelming – it is all the minister can do to get some quiet in order to begin the short baptismal service. Throughout some chatter persists, and the flashing of cameras gives the impression more of a press conference than a church service. A few hangers-on from the previous Eucharist make the responses, and do their best with a hymn. The gathered family and friends of this dashingly dressed three-year-old baptisand seem oblivious to these efforts; not even the Lord's Prayer is entered into. Not unreasonably, I suppose, as no one seems to know it, and it hasn't been copied out for them.

And, as the parents promise to raise this child in the faith of the Church, and as the sign of the light of Christ is given her, a thought crosses the minds of one or two parishioners, myself included: Well, of course, the local Christian school is over-subscribed ... A concern grows about what, exactly, is going on here.

In the following weeks and months, many in the parish look out for this family which has been incorporated into the life of Jesus Christ, both at church and in the town. They are not seen again.

STORY 3: A BAPTISM OF GROWN-UP CONVERSION

Many in the parish have known Catherine in her months of preparation for this night, and have been blessed by this knowing of her. From her first tentative enquiries in coming to the church, through her time of learning and praying with other Christians, the small congregation has been graced with glimpses of the Holy Spirit at work in her life, past and present. She has celebrated with the community the deep mysteries of Holy Week, when the Lord's love at the Last Supper is vividly proclaimed, and the way of the cross is followed.

It is dark outside, and the great celebration of the Easter vigil, with its dawning light of hundreds of candles, and its solemn proclamation of our salvation through readings from Scripture, has fed the minds and senses of all present. This is a night of newness, resurrected life, a foretaste of the glory to which we are all called in Jesus.

And it is here, in the heart of this celebration, that this 37-year-old woman will be baptised – with some embarrassment, needless to say, but with conviction, and joy, and laughter. Head wet with fragrant oil and damp with the new waters of baptism, Catherine is led down the church, and greeted over and over with the peace of Christ. She is the first, after the ministers, to receive the Eucharist this night, and she becomes, in her own personal and particular way, a reminder of the call to Jesus that is true for all Christians, however long ago we may have lost sight of it, or however dull it has lately become to our ears. This new Christian life, this particular person's sharing in the death and resurrection of Jesus in baptism and Eucharist – this rightly stands at the heart of the celebration of Easter; for it is, in essence, the very celebration of the whole of Christian faith and its call upon the baptised person.

The party after the two-and-a-half-hour service goes on into this 'night truly blessed',[9] *and, for once, it seems entirely right to be drinking champagne and rejoicing before the cross of Christ.*

Catherine's life in Christ begins in a new way this night, and as the months and years go on, she grows in her own vocation among her friends (and enemies! – we are an imperfect community, after all) in the parish, and among the people she works with and meets. The people of God are blessed with another teacher, another healer, another intercessor for the life of the Church and the world.

QUESTIONS ARISING

For some of us more 'churchy' people, these stories pose tricky and perennial questions: Who should be baptised? How can we judge? Who should be responsible? How should the baptismal celebration be carried out, and when? Does the baptism of the child in the unchurched family make any difference? How? But these rather ecclesiastical preoccupations are symptoms of a more profound and important question, which is common to these examples of the practice of baptism: *What is going on?!* Only when we begin to focus on this more basic question can all those others find a proper place.

This fundamental question – *What is going on?!* – is also the necessary basis for all the other, 'non-churchy' questions about baptism. After all, however pressing to the 'professionals' questions of baptismal practice and policy might seem, it is clear, too, that questions arise from 'outside' the visible boundaries of the Christian community. The baptised person who has no experience of church life or teaching, has often some fairly important questions of their own: Did that long-ago infant ritual mean anything? Could it really make any difference to me now? What were my parents thinking? But I don't *want* to be a Christian! Then there is the non-churchgoing, uncatechised parent seeking baptism for their child: Why shouldn't this child have the benefit? What right have you to deprive him? Are you saying she's not good enough?

Wherever we start out looking at the practice of baptism, questions trouble us; and these varied, often painful questions, return us to the one question of baptismal theology – *What is going on?* The very practice of baptism, when we look at it seriously and thoughtfully, challenges us to look beyond the church celebration to something altogether less manageable, more complicated, and full of life: that is, living as a follower of Jesus Christ in the world.

It is in the very nature of baptism as both a mystery of God's action and a 'thing done' by fallible, not always very nice people, that this questioning is inevitable. The questions abound further when, culturally, this mysterious 'thing done' has become, for many, a done thing, as in much of our own 'post-Christian' culture. But these questions are not new to the Christian tradition, and we need to recognise that, for 2000 years, people have not only done baptism, but have reflected on, thought about, and brought their best gifts of intellect and grace to bear on the questions. We are not without answers in our Christian memory – albeit partial ones. What, perhaps, we *have* often been without, is the time and opportunity and wisdom to be attentive to that long tradition of holy learning, and allow it to shape our lives. This is the challenge that faces our difficult doing and living of baptism today.

CHAPTER TWO

BAPTISM AND THE RESHAPING OF 'CHURCH'

> *... like living stones let yourselves be built into a spiritual house, to be a holy priesthood, to offer spiritual sacrifices to God through Jesus Christ ...* 1 Peter 2:5

One of the traditional ways in which Christians have answered that central question of baptism, *What is going on here?*, is by reference to the Christian community itself, the Church. Baptism makes new members of the Church, new sons and daughters of God's family in Christ.[1] Indeed, it has become common to talk of baptism as a 'rite of initiation' into the Christian life, embodied in the Church as the Christian community. But if this is an obvious answer to what happens in baptism, it is also rather problematic. Our interpretation of it depends entirely on what we think is meant by 'Church': is this simply an organisation, membership of which is secured through the rite of baptism? Is Church a purely mystical, and rather vague community of the blessed, which has no real, concrete links with my life? Or is it only to be found in the thorough 'churchiness' of liturgies, parish activities, prayer groups and committees? If baptism is a rite of initiation, what, in fact, are we initiated into?

As a basis for what follows about the living of baptism, this chapter sets out to do two things. The first is to establish the idea that baptism is not so much a 'rite of passage' into a particular community, but more the source and root and fount of renewal and recreation of the Church itself. The Church, in its structural and organisational life, both depends upon, and is set up to serve, the living of baptism. The baptismal life in the world is a fundamental and integral part of what Church is, whether or not it looks 'churchy'.

As a second point, following on from this idea, it will be suggested that it is precisely this renewed sense of the Church as based on baptismal living – a 'baptismal ecclesiology' – which is really needed today. In order to respond more deeply and appropriately to the contemporary world, renewed living of Church must be found, above all a living rooted in baptismal vocation and theology. We don't so much need better management, better PR, better marketing in the Christian community, so much as we need faithful and vibrant living of the mystery of baptism. We want, in all this discussion, to take on the adventure of nurturing the ordinary living of baptism. In doing this we are, in fact, concerning ourselves with the renewal of the Church in a fundamental and necessary way.

Central to this is the realisation that the living of baptism is not a churchy, ecclesiastical affair, but something much more 'ordinary'. Thinking back to the doing of baptism, what I mean can be put like this: at the end of the service of baptism we leave the church, we go out of the church building; but we also take Christ's Church out with us, as Christian disciples, because we ourselves have been made living members of Church in our baptism. The *living* of baptism – which flows out from the *event* – has, as its proper place, 'the world', the ordinary, human places of daily life. The Church is not only a structured, human-looking organisation of religion, but is also (and must be) the explicit and continuing presence of Christ in the world, through the living of his disciples, who share his life in baptism. Being the Church is every bit as much about being 'in the world' as it is to do with being 'in church'.[2] It is this that a full and liveable theology of baptism has the potential to teach us. Baptised Christians are, in the main, called to holy living in the ordinariness of society – a living 'in ordinary', which is made extraordinary by the baptismal promise that we are, in Christ, all called to eternal life in heaven with God.

The difficulty for many of us is that baptism and Church seem – well, 'churchy'! Sometimes it is hard to remember, in any effective way, that the great realities that baptism tells us about and really draws us into sharing, are not only things to marvel at in church; they are not realities reserved for our religious, pious selves, whenever that persona is called into play for some reason. No. These baptismal mysteries are to be discovered, and understood more deeply, and lived out, in our ordinary, 'worldly' lives. As a baptised person I can't go in and out of church; rather, I am always, and everywhere, called to fully participate in Christ's body, the Church, in communion with everyone else who shares this baptism. It is the building up of that sense of lay living of Church, or Christian discipleship, in the ordinariness of the world, that we need to establish as the theological basis of our reflections on baptism.

CHRISTIAN DISCIPLESHIP TODAY: WHAT IS NEEDED?

By raising the question of the Church here, we are brought face to face with certain real-life difficulties. In particular, in our late-modern, Western society, we are often made aware of the 'post-Christian' nature of our context: the Church can no longer assume an unquestioned voice and authority in society at large; nor can it even assume that its traditional language will be understood. Church attendance and active involvement are dropping, and the churches themselves have tended to become preoccupied by their own survival and identity.

This presents us with a danger. An over-anxiety about the Church in her present context can all too easily bring about a wrong focus – a focus on maintenance, rather than mission; on structures rather than living; on organisation and polity, rather than ordinary living in Christ. Here, those 'liberation theologies' which have grown out of the situations of oppression in Latin America have something to teach us.[3] In particular, when these liberation theologians write about Church, and about sacraments and liturgies, they can often sound very critical, even, sometimes, as if they didn't care, very much, for the structures and traditions of Church. But this critical voice alerts us to something important: Christians, faced with the terrible difficulties of society, and the pressures on their community, retreat into looking at their own 'internal', ecclesiastical affairs – and it is this withdrawal into a maintenance sense of Church that liberation theologies are so critical of. For such an introverted way of being Church is not, usually, much good to anyone out there who is suffering the tragedies of the world. We busy ourselves with these 'domestic' anxieties, fussing, like so many Marthas, about things that – to the rest of the world – seem far from needful.[4] As the moral theologian and priest, Enda McDonagh, observes when writing about Eucharist:

> In a world threatened by human destructiveness militarily and ecologically, agreed statements on the Eucharist and even the development of inter-church celebrations may appear trivial and peripheral. The formal domus Dei [household of God] must lift its eyes to the gifts and needs of the whole world about it, the mundus Dei [world of God], if it would truly worship God.[5]

In a world of real need and anguish, the Church of Jesus Christ is called to more than liturgies and happy gatherings and reorganisation. It must learn to be prophetic and missionary.

Well, of course, the 'internal' and the 'external' to the Church are not so very clearly defined and distinct as such a criticism might first appear to suggest. Nonetheless, we are warned by these sensitivities against any overly introverted concern with Christian sacraments – especially, perhaps, that of baptism. The challenge here is to lift our eyes away from fonts, and white garments, and candles, for a moment, in order to gaze more steadily and honestly at our world. For this is the world from which, and into which, all the baptised are called, as ambassadors of the world to come.

What is set before our eyes here is too complex, too varied, too many-layered, and just plain painful for me to give any really satisfactory account of it. Cultural commentators and philosophers debate the various movements in thinking and perceiving of our own time and place, variously describing it all as post-modern, late-modern, post-Christian and so forth; and we can be overwhelmed by the sheer complexity of all this.[6] However, there are a few things which seem to be central and commonly observed facets of our social reality to which we can usefully refer.

In the West we enjoy a relative comfort and security which is without precedent in human history. The easy access I have to a whole world of food and drink, and to electricity, warmth, water and entertainment is breathtaking. Much of this is built on inexcusable exploitation of the poorest of the world, for whom hope of enough to eat, clean water, and basic health care is often all but lost. Still, I enjoy this safe and pleasant place; and I am thoroughly implicated in the injustices it brings about and requires for its continuance.

Our European culture can also be seen as both post-modern and post-Christian (or, more accurately, post-Christendom). Any earlier modern optimism based on the supposed certainties or authorities of science and technology has been thoroughly shaken. Post-modern men and women are left with a less sure framework for understanding their world; we can choose from a pluralism of world-views, philosophies and faiths, and even pick and mix from these to make up our own solutions. The earlier-still sureties of a commonly held Christian faith seem just about completely absent from the public culture and language of our societies.

We may know material well-being in extraordinary and historically new ways; but we seem no nearer making any sense of it all, and less likely than ever to find something we can really put our trust in, or commit our lives to.

From a Christian perspective, this situation has most commonly been seen as one crying out for *mission*, for *evangelisation*. For Pope John Paul II this was a common theme throughout his writings, as he describes a world longing for redemption and hope, in which love, and truth, and security are barely visible to men and women. The very creativity and technological advance of people brings about a world where human beings live in fear of what they themselves have made.[7] Underpinning this is a fundamental loss of meaning, and a loss of hope for coming generations:

> ... it is undeniable that this time of rapid and complex change can leave especially the younger generation, to whom the future belongs and on whom it depends, with a sense that they have no valid points of reference. The need for a foundation for personal and communal life becomes all the more pressing at a time when we are faced with the patent inadequacy of perspectives in which the ephemeral is affirmed as a value and the possibility of discovering the real meaning of life is cast into doubt. This is why many people stumble through life to the very edge of the abyss without knowing where they are going.[8]

It is into such a world, and this sense of having lost the way, that the Christian message today is to speak. Men and women, our neighbours, friends and family, are often living life in 'quiet desperation', at some level haunted by that sense of the abyss that lies just a little way from their path.

And here we are, us Christians, fussing about the domestic matter of baptism, and the survival of the church organisation!

Thus the question arises: the baptism thing, given the world as it is – is this the 'one thing needful'?[9] Can baptism be an adequate response to what we see when we look at the world around us? Can this strange water ceremony do any good?

Well, yes and no. For underlying the many, niggling questions about baptism – some important, some less so – is the radiant and extraordinary Christian faith concerning redemption and discipleship. It is *this* which is the true subject of baptism; the living and joyful hope of Christian discipleship. And *this* is, indeed, the thing needed! For what the Christian tradition tells us is that it is here, in baptism, that the evangelising heart of the Gospel – the life, death and resurrection of Jesus – becomes a living and lived reality in our own time and place. This is the mystery of redemption – the mystery of broken, wandering, lost human beings being found, and 'saved' and (above all) *loved completely*, by the One who alone is able to do this. It is just this mystery which is brought to light and life in the day-to-day and ordinary, by baptism. Baptism is absolutely what is needed in today's world; but it is the baptism that is *lived*, and not the rituals alone.

This radical understanding of baptism and its power to change lives, and societies, is essential to understanding and carrying out the life and mission of the Church. So it is that an authority of the international Anglican Communion is able to place baptism at the heart of the Christian call to mission:

> During this decade of evangelisation [this report] presents a ground-plan for the renewal of the church in mission and ministry and places the baptismal life of the church at the heart of its vocation to service in the world.[10]

It is precisely a focus on the living of baptism, rather than on church structures, that can enable the Church to be truly missionary, and a sign and promise of hope to the world. This is what we mean primarily when we speak of 'Church' here – the living of baptism in the world, and for the service and good of others. How we are to make this a true and effective part of our lives is the question we must face, and the challenge to which we must rise, if we are to stop Christ's Church just being a churchy organisation or club.

TEMPTATIONS TO 'FIX' THE CHURCH

The rediscovery – and living – of baptism as the heart of the Christian Church is urgent and necessary, especially in the light of these observations. But it also requires a radical shift in thinking for most people – Christians and non-Christians – about what the Church is, what actually constitutes it as Church. This needs some explaining.

One of the things that happens whenever any organisation feels a bit shaky, or under threat, is that it seeks to 'fix' itself. This 'fixing' carries a double meaning, which is quite deliberate. First of all, clearly, there is the sense in which a troubled or disintegrating human community seeks to be mended, to put things right. It may need to adapt, to alter its 'mission statement', change its image, or get rid of redundant structures. These things may well mend apparent breaches and threats to the organisation. They also, and at the same time, 'fix' an organisation, in the sense of pinning it down to something, making it more concrete, more identifiable.

Something like this can be discerned in the contemporary Western Church. When theologians and pastors turn their minds and efforts to the Church – when they do ecclesiology – they recognise certain problems, certain troubles and anxieties about the Church. Some of these difficulties are most visible in the maintenance of structures; others are about the vitality and life of the Church and her mission. The temptation is to treat the Church as if it were like any other organisation and work out how to 'fix' (mend) things, in ways which generally involve 'fixing' (pinning down) the Church. In particular, we like to think we've got this Church well managed, under control – *our* control, that is.

The problem is that the Christian Church is 'the body of Christ',[11] the mystery which communicates salvation to the world.[12] This faith in the Church means that the Church is radically *not like* other organisations, and so needs to be worked with rather differently. What this means is not altogether clear, and has always been a problem for the Christian understanding of Church. So we will tend to go with the dominant culture, and want to manage, 'fix', sort out this troublesome organisation of Church. We will seek to manage the Church's difficulties by making the mystery manageable, by attempting to take control ourselves of God's mission and future, by acting as though *we* were in charge of Church, and not the Holy Spirit. Above all, we make the mistake of thinking that the Church's political, organisational reality (important as it is) is the primary, even the *only*, reality of Church. To do this is to forget the living of the graces of baptism – a living often hidden from strategic and managerial accounts of Church life.

There are a number of prominent examples of this 'fixing' of Church to which we might refer. Preoccupations with structures of governance and authority; pastoral plans for diocese and parishes; a concentration on the liturgical and ritual; the ubiquitous insistence on the Church as 'community' – each of these, in their different ways, seeks, with generally good intentions, to put right the troubled contemporary Church by 'fixing' it, getting it sorted and defined in ways that make it manageable.

An ecclesiology, or theology of Church, based on baptism is, in relation to these trends, something of a conscious *unfixing* of Church. It is a radical shift of trust, a letting go of our own plans and strategies, so as to let something bigger, something of God, take hold.

BAPTISM AS A UNIVERSAL CALL TO HOLINESS

The point in all this is that, as a necessary beginning to our reflections on the particular aspects of baptismal living, we need to be clear that the call to be Church is *not* (for most of us) a call to be churchy or ecclesiastical. Our theology of baptism is required, more and more, to challenge those notions of Church which focus unduly on the structural, organisational, political life of the Christian community; for baptism reminds us that Christian discipleship is lived – if it is lived at all – 'in ordinary'. The future and present health of the Church cannot, in the light of baptism, be the responsibility of leaders, committees and hierarchies alone, but is, primarily, the vocation of each baptised person, and of all together. The much-talked-of 'renewal' of the Church is, in the light of a baptism-based view of Church, to be understood as the rebirth of the Church from the hearts of men and women.[13]

One of the (smaller!) low points of my time working in parish pastoral work was when, after a long team meeting discussing the shape and content of some adult catechesis on the mysterious and awesome sacrament of baptism, our parish priest yawned loudly and said, 'Couldn't we choose another topic? To be honest, I just think baptism is *so boring*!' And I'm pretty sure that – on some level – he meant it. Once I'd managed to put aside my frustration and irritation at such an unconstructive contribution to the work in hand, I was able to think more clearly on what was genuinely problematic in this expression of clerical boredom with baptism.

For me, the shocking nature of this remark was that it appeared to reduce to the level of the mundane and irrelevant that very mystery which describes, informs and gives life to my Christian vocation precisely as a lay woman, a 'woman of the world'! It sat in my memory – and still sits there – as a symptom of so much of what is 'wrong with the Church' in our own time and place. It is a candid moment in discussion which demonstrates how far we have to go in fully appropriating ideas of living baptism. For the cleric, perhaps over-burdened with questions of baptismal policy and liturgies, baptism does, indeed, become boring: a ritual, a difficulty, an administration. For me, trying to live my baptism day to day, it is more about discipleship, the universal vocation to holiness, being called to life with God, and the mission to express God's love for the world. This is not, I think, boring. But we still tend to think of 'the Church' as a more-or-less clerical organisation, a set of structures to be maintained, systems to be staffed and resourced; and such a view renders baptism a tedious, dull question of policy and practice. A full and lived theology of baptism can free us from this over-institutional reading of Church and Christ's people.

To call for a renewed sense of the Church as baptismally formed and orientated, is to remind ourselves of the fundamental significance of a theology of 'lay', or non-clerical, un-churchy, Christian living. By this I don't mean a concern for how lay people can do more in the Church, or exercise 'lay ministries'. Rather, I am referring to the general, 'ordinary' living of Christian life, thoroughly in the world.

It is the sensitivity to this 'universal vocation to holiness', as

Vatican II calls it,[14] which lies behind the choice of the verse from 1 Peter which heads this chapter. It is a curious verse, which repays study. Its curiosity is presented to us in the use of a blatantly mixed metaphor – the odd, nonsensical idea of 'living stones'. As a way of describing a reality, clearly this doesn't quite work, on one level; stones are, evidently, anything but 'living', and it is not at all clear how we might imagine a 'living stone' to be. It is nonsense. But as a way of speaking of the mystery of the Church as *both* structural *and*, fundamentally, to do with life in Christ, this works perfectly. The image illustrates the way in which the Church is both something to be maintained, and also, always, something much more than that – something which grows mysteriously in the power of Christ's life among us. A similar image is found in Ephesians:

> You are citizens with the saints and also members of the household of God, built upon the foundation of the apostles and prophets, with Christ Jesus himself as the cornerstone. In him the whole structure is joined together and grows into a holy temple in the Lord; in whom you also are built together spiritually into a dwelling place for God.[15]

Stones which live and grow, organic-sounding buildings ... these strange images, taking their sense from life in Christ, speak about what it is to be Church.

Overwhelmingly, too, these speak about what it is to be Church 'in ordinary'. In 1 Peter the context is clearly one of exhorting ordinary Christians to holiness of life. The concern is not with church services as such, but with the offering of 'spiritual sacrifices', the daily offering of life to God which enables it to be graced and gifted by God. Christians are not straightforwardly called in these texts to gather in church buildings, or to form organisations, but rather to be built up, by a power beyond themselves, into 'a spiritual house' – something which transcends the merely material and structural.

Here are some beginnings for a theology of lay discipleship, that common living of baptism which characterises Church at its heart.[16] It is a theology of Church which, above all, centres on the transformed and transforming living of baptism, naming this as the primary reality of Church, to which all structures and projects are ordered in service. It is this profound ecclesial sense of baptism which led St Augustine to speak of his own baptism, in the context of his office as bishop (or overseer) of the Church:

> The fact that I am a Christian is for my benefit; that I am appointed an overseer is for yours. My own good is to be considered in my being a Christian; in my being an overseer, only yours.[17]

It is baptism, the beginning of Christian life, which is the real grace of Christian discipleship, and our one great gift in Christ. Office and ministry in the Church are always ordered to the general life of baptism; it is *for* the people, not for the office-holder. There are, of course, structures, ministries and tasks in the Church. But what unites them and keeps them on the right track together, is that common call of baptism. The task of the whole Church is the full living of baptism, in and for the world.

THE CHURCH CENTRED ON ITS MARGINS

To seek, as we do here, to reinterpret what we mean by 'Church' in terms of the ordinary living of baptism is to highlight a certain permanent tension in ecclesial life. On one level this is the Gospel tension of being 'in the world, and not of the world':[18] Christian witness is both ordinary and extraordinary, both like and unlike other human beliefs and activity. We are here reaffirming that tradition of Christian life which sees as pre-eminently Church that mysterious communion of saints, here on earth, in ordinary living, together with the company of heaven. The ordinary living of sanctity in the world is often a hidden, obscure affair. It is of this that the 'ordinary' or 'common' sacrament of baptism speaks when it tells us about Church.

To say, in the light of this, that Church is primarily about living baptism 'in ordinary' is to challenge some more normal ways of thinking about Church. In particular, this idea of baptism challenges the organisational centre and sense of the ecclesial structures, from the places which *appear* at the edges of Church life, at least in terms of structures. For there is a sense in which lay living of discipleship is *both* central to Church, *and*, at the same time, on the edge.

What I mean here is most clearly evidenced in an organisationally hierarchical church such as the Roman Catholic Church. Here it is customary, for example, in 'official' and papal letters to address the church as a whole from the bishops 'down', through the ranks of clergy, and consecrated religious, to the mass of lay men and women. Lay people are, organisationally, it seems, the bottom of the heap! Nor is this simply some oppressive hierarchical reading, peculiar to Roman Catholicism; in different ways there is an inevitable sense in which ecclesial organisations are centred around the ministers, the 'professionals', maybe with some lay representatives. It is in the nature of the lay living of Christian discipleship that there are just too many other, everyday things going on for the majority to be able (or willing) to give large amounts of time to the church organisation. Lay vocation is, almost by definition, on the 'edges' of church organisation.

Once we fully appropriate the truth that it is baptism which fundamentally shapes and calls the Church into life, something happens to this reading of the 'edges' and 'centre' of the Church. A baptismally oriented ecclesiology sets out to affirm *both* the proper 'secularity' of lay living, *and*, at the same time, its proper nature as the normal, central aspect of the Church's living of the call to holiness in Christ. The baptismal vocation 'in ordinary' is, simultaneously, the margins *and* the centre of Church life; and it is so because the nature of Christ's Church (*unlike* other organisations) is not primarily to do with institutional survival, but with making the world – the edges of 'Church' – the focus, the centre, of loving attention.

This call to love the world – or rather, to communicate God's love to a world in need – this is, necessarily, a centring on the margins. And it is in responding to this as the vocation of Christian discipleship that we can return to baptismal living as properly the heart of Church life and mission. It is precisely the ordinariness of the way in which baptism is most commonly lived out, in the world, in families, at work, in popular culture – it is this which makes it the true root of any Church renewal, or evangelising efforts.

So it is that the renewal of the Church (much needed), and the hope of the world (so allusive) are to be born – not from ecclesial programmes and projects, but from those places where baptism is being fully lived in the lives of 'ordinary' men and women.

CHAPTER THREE

THE TRADITION OF BAPTISM AS VOCATION

> *... and it is no longer I who live, but it is Christ who lives in me. And the life I now live in the flesh I live by faith in the Son of God, who loved me and gave himself for me.* Galatians 2:20

I have suggested, so far, that there has been altogether too much energy and interest put into the discussion of baptismal rituals, liturgies and policies. For all the rhetoric of baptism being at the heart of the life and mission of Christian communities, most people – baptised or not – see baptism primarily, or simply, as an occasion, an event, that happens and then is done. We might have an idea that baptism makes us members of the Church, but our very understanding of what that means is often insubstantial or distorted. The organisational churches themselves have run the risk of seeing baptism too politically, too ritualistically, too culturally. In so far as we have fallen into that danger, as baptised people, we have failed to live the power and mystery gifted to us in this sacrament. What is now being looked to is a radical reorientation towards a living of Church in the day-to-day call of our baptism.

This sounds such a daunting project! And yet, as this chapter hopes to set out, the perennial liveliness and freshness of the mystery that is the baptismal life persists. It is a source of hope for Christians, and for the whole world.

The problem is, it seems to me, that we only really feel on safe ground when we can talk of baptism in its ecclesiastical, canonical, liturgical, ritual, and policy aspects. Baptism as something concrete, a doing of the Church – and a relatively simple doing at that – is something we can deal with, legislate for, develop programmes about. When we decide, as I am deciding now, to leave that socio-ecclesiastical security behind, due to its sheer dullness and failure to give life, we turn aside and set our sights on less well-trodden paths. The adventure ahead is one of the exploration of baptism as a life-giving gift, as mission, as the way of Christian life. This is, I have suggested, a necessary, even urgent adventure, if baptism is to rediscover its place at the heart of the Gospel message of discipleship, and so renew the life of the Church, and of the whole world.

If this is a path that is less well trodden than other, more conventional contemporary studies of baptism, it is, nonetheless, *not* a barren wilderness or an alien planet. Many of the richest treasures of the Christian tradition of study and prayer and wisdom for living have, when we look more closely, been concerned to spell out and give song to the baptismal life as the most profound reality of living for the Christian. These treasures shall be our guiding lights and sounds in what follows. For now, what will be important is to establish clearly what it might mean to consider baptism in this way: not simply as event, but as call; not as ritual only, but as way of life; not as 'rite of passage', but doorway into the disturbing world of grace, with its radically new ways of being human.[1] To do this we will look at a number of persistent themes in theologies and meditations on baptism, from across the Christian generations, and across denominational and traditional divides. In all of this we will begin to be attuned to the theological and prayerful whisperings concerning the truth about baptism as a living power and grace in our lives, and in the world.

THE BAPTISMAL THEMES OF SCRIPTURE

The rich testimony of Scripture to the baptismal life will be our constant point of return and renewal. Learning how to live baptism is, in large part, about learning our living out of Scripture. Here we learn how to walk in the ways in which the Word calls us in those books, and it is the exploration of these ways in thought and prayer which is the central concern of the chapters that follow. For now we will only remind ourselves of the shape of what is spoken about baptism in the New Testament. And it is about 'shape' rather than any single doctrinal statement; for, above all, the New Testament provides us with a rich cluster of images of baptism, and an extraordinary narrative of baptismal practice. The rich treasury of imagery is referred to succinctly (though not exhaustively) in the World Council of Churches' Faith and Order paper on baptism:

> Baptism is a participation in Christ's death and resurrection (Rom. 6:3–5; Col. 2:2); a washing away of sin (1 Cor. 6:11); a new birth (John 3:5); an enlightenment by Christ (Eph. 5:14); a reclothing in Christ (Gal. 3:27); a renewal by the Spirit (Titus 3:5); the experience of salvation from the flood (1 Pet. 3:20–21); an exodus from bondage (1 Cor. 10:1–2); and a liberation into a new humanity in which barriers of division ... are transcended (Gal. 3:27; 1 Cor. 12:13).[2]

All this – and more – the Scriptures want to teach us about baptism. We see, too, in the scriptural stories the ways in which the action of baptism is the consistent response of those who come to hear about and believe in Jesus' teaching, and his saving death and resurrection.[3] Baptism is the answer to the question of faith, which asks, on hearing the story of Jesus Christ, 'What should we do?'

In all this, the New Testament presents us with baptism as new life, as the naming of conversion of life. Baptism is seen as a *turning point*. What we will not find anywhere in the New Testament is any apparent interest in 'the rite of baptism', or in any 'liturgical theology' concerning this practice. Yet, again and again, baptism appears as a critical event, after which nothing is the same again. As a *point* of change it is almost invisible – a speck in the drama of Gospel and apostolic preaching, occupying little space; but as a point of *turning* baptism patterns and shapes and orientates that drama, pointing always beyond itself to the life that is to be grown out of it.

The 'turning around' nature of baptism is clear from its earliest Christian roots in the baptism preached and practised by John, and undergone by the Lord himself. This is, after all, a baptism 'of repentance';[4] in the Greek, a baptism of *metanoia* or 'revolution of outlook'. To approach the waters of John's baptism is to seek forgiveness, a 'letting go' (*aphiemi*) of past faults, regrets, sins, so as to start anew in eager anticipation of the coming of the Kingdom. Although we cannot see Jesus as seeking forgiveness as such, we can clearly see Jesus' own baptism as a new beginning, the start of his ministry and Passion, which is the real substance of the Gospel story that follows this moment. At the point of Jesus' baptism we glimpse something of the mystery of the Trinity, the Spirit's descending, the love and confidence of the Father for the Son.[5] And it is from this peep into the divine mystery that Jesus is pushed out into his public ministry.[6] The baptism of the Lord is over in a few verses, but that brief sighting of God in Jesus acts powerfully throughout the many chapters that follow.

Indeed, there are one or two significant moments where this sense of the turning point of baptism surfaces clearly in Jesus' own life. In particular, the Gospel writers report Jesus' use of the language of baptism to describe his coming suffering and death. This seems to be what is envisaged by Luke when, in the middle of some hard and urgent teaching on the coming Kingdom, he writes how Jesus recognises in himself and his teaching a sign of contradiction, of division, conflict, even:

> I came to bring fire to the earth, and how I wish it were already kindled! I have a baptism with which to be baptised, and what stress I am under until it is completed![7]

Something similar can be sensed when Jesus challenges his ambitious followers: 'Can you be baptised with the baptism that I am baptised with?'[8] The suggestion from most commentaries is that this refers to Jesus' coming suffering and death, through which alone his 'power and glory' – which so concern James and John here – will be manifest and established. In the end it is the turning point of the cross to which this language of baptism refers us; it is Christ's eternal 'letting go' (*aphiemi*, forgiveness) of sin in death and resurrection that is, literally, the *crux* (cross) of the matter of baptism.

What we are just catching sight of here is the complex way in which the baptism of John, for the forgiveness of sin, is most powerfully understood in the Gospels as a turning around to live in new ways, pointing to a new future (God's). Jesus' own baptism marks the starting point of his saving ministry, which is also a point of departure, of going out and away, into a living which draws him to the cross. 'You are my Son, the Beloved; with you I am well pleased.'[9] In the brief moment of baptism the Father speaks and enacts his love for the Son, and Jesus is sent out into the future. Baptism is the small event which is the beginning of the great drama of salvation.

What the Gospel narratives mainly speak of when talking of baptism, is the baptism of John, a baptism of repentance for the forgiveness of sins, a turning point in preparation for the coming of the Lord himself. But there is always the promise of something greater – of baptism through Jesus, in (or by) the Holy Spirit: 'I baptise you with water for repentance, but one who is more powerful than I is coming after me ... He will baptise you with the Holy Spirit and with fire.'[10] It is this baptism, filled with the power of the resurrection and of the Holy Spirit, that is opened up to believers through the cross and new life of Jesus, risen from the dead.

In Acts and the letters of St Paul, it is this baptism, 'into Christ' or 'in the name of the Lord Jesus', which is the transforming and shaping power of all that takes place, and of all that we are called to. Like the baptism of John described in the Gospel, this too is a tiny point, a *moment* of turning and transformation. With this perspective it is less surprising to read the rather abrupt and stark accounts of baptisms given in Acts, whether of the thousands who wish to respond to Peter's proclamation of the news about Jesus,[11] or of Cornelius' Gentile household, which is already 'baptised by the Spirit',[12] or of Lydia,[13] or Simon[14] or any of the other first Christians. What is always given more space is the proclamation of the Good News, the response of faith, and the transformation of life that follows.

It is for this reason of emphasis, also, that we find in Paul's letters reference to baptism as a *reminder* – a way of calling his erring flock's attention to what they have already become, in Christ (*en Christo* – a favourite phrase of St Paul's, full of baptismal referent). The memory of baptism is made to speak of how we are to live, here and now. So, it is because we are baptised that there should be no divisions among us[15] – we are 'baptised into one body' where there are no divisions of race or status.[16] Indeed, such a transformation is undergone in baptism, that the Christian can be said to 'have put on Christ', becoming a 'new creation'.[17] What is of concern to Paul in all these passages is the life that is being lived in the power of baptism (or not), rather than the doings of baptisms.

Indeed, the opening chapter of 1 Corinthians can be read as composed in a somewhat irritated tone, as Paul berates the Christians of Corinth for attaching too much importance to who baptised them, or who their baptism connects them to.[18] This is an overemphasis on the event itself. What is important, Paul stresses, is that there is only baptism into Christ, and Christ cannot be divided. He then says something rather striking about his own ministry of bringing people to Christ:

> I thank God that I baptised none of you except Crispus and Gaius, so that no one can say that you were baptised in my name ... For Christ did not send me to baptise but to proclaim the Gospel, and not with eloquent wisdom, so that the cross of Christ might not be emptied of its power.[19]

What follows this assertion is Paul's beautiful reflection on the message of Christ's cross, as the wisdom of God, whilst scandal and folly to men and women.

It is as if Paul's frustrations over some kind of row tied up with baptismal polity and status push him to look beyond these ecclesiastical doings to the greater and more real mystery: Christ's love and saving death for us. The references to baptism as *event* kick the Apostle's thinking out into the future promised us by God, in Christ. What remains important is this call to us, and our living out of it, turned to God's future. In this we are grown up out of the grace of Christ's death and resurrection in which, mysteriously, we come to share in baptism.[20] It is the presence of this mystery in our transformed, 'ordinary' living which is the uniting and empowering fact of Christian life for Paul.

MARKED FOR LIFE

We have seen that the scriptural witness is most concerned with the living out of baptism, as a turning point of faith. This ongoing sacramental sense is present in other parts of the long Christian tradition of thinking about baptism. One of the ways in which the every-day-ness of baptism has been spoken of in the Christian tradition subsequent to the composition of the books of the New Testament is through the often problematic language of 'sacramental character', or by the use of 'ontological' language.[21] So we find stated in the Catechism of the Catholic Church:

> Baptism imprints on the soul an indelible spiritual sign, the character, which consecrates the person for Christian worship. Because of the character Baptism cannot be repeated.[22]

Here it is understood that something happens in baptism which 'marks' us, forever and on the deepest level of our being (the level of 'ontology'). Our soul is stamped by God – once and for all.

Whatever we make of this in the future, it was God's doing and so has permanent effect – at least as far as he is concerned!

This language can, at first, trouble us with difficult questions. How can a soul be 'marked' (even 'spiritually')? How can baptism make a permanent, real difference when we can choose to ignore or abandon it, when we can't recall it, when it means nothing to us? Aren't we all too sophisticated in this contemporary culture of ours to want to speak of souls being stamped by God, as if baptism was like getting a visa? But there is richness in this tradition which needs further reflection.

The idea of baptism 'marking' us has a long history. The reference above is to a contemporary authority on Roman Catholic teaching, with which this idea is most commonly associated; but as far back as Tertullian in the second century, the scriptural language of a 'seal' was adopted as a way of speaking of what was done in baptism. By the time of Augustine (fifth century) there is a growing consensus about the use of such terms. It is, though, in the writings of St Thomas Aquinas that this idea is most systematically developed.

For Aquinas baptism is the way in which God, through human actions in the liturgy, gives men and women the extraordinary gift needed for true worship. It is in baptism that we are deputed to the handing on and receiving of holy things, the things to do with the divine life.[23] Baptismal 'character' is the way in which we understand this sacramental marking, which gives us the spiritual competence (*potestas spiritualis*) to take part in the Church's life of worship of God through Christ, and in the Spirit. We can only participate in this extraordinary commerce with the divine through God's own act upon our being – his marking of us with the sacramental character of baptism.

It would be a mistake, I think, to read this sense of the commissioning of sacramental character in too limited a sense of 'divine worship'. For Aquinas, this worship of God is our participation in Christ, life in the Spirit, which, whilst expressed in a particular and sure way in the Church's liturgy, is not simply a matter of ritual. Rather, the whole of human life is to be taken up into the call of the Church to prayer, virtue, holiness. It is for this that the sacramental character of baptism marks us out.

Much more could be said about the historical development of this language of 'character'. For some it looks clearly like a deviation from Scripture, and an over-complicated philosophical embellishment of the 'simple' Gospel message and practice. For others it reads more like a mystical deepening of our understanding of this great mystery in which, St Paul tells us, we become a new creation and stand as 'co-heirs' with Christ.[24] What is important for us is the way in which this language of 'mark' and 'character' – still very much a part of the living Christian tradition – struggles to express certain true things about baptism. In particular, it tells us things which have profound importance for our understanding of baptism as vocation and way of life. This tradition speaks eloquently of baptism as a permanent promise of gift from God, to be borne and lived.[25]

For to say that in baptism we receive a 'character' or 'mark' or 'seal' on our deepest being, which 'configures us to Christ',[26] is to recognise at a most profound level the constancy and 'living' nature of this sacrament. It is after the liturgy, after the service, when we go home, go to work, go to parties and know that we bear within ourselves this act of God, which has marked us for himself – it is then, in our living of life, that we know most fully the reality that baptism is and brings about. Just as the event of the birth of my baby is both truly event *par excellence*, and the beginning of a whole new life, and a whole new way of life; just as, after the wedding and the honeymoon, something new and scary and day-to-day is to begin; just like this, God's act upon us in baptism is an extraordinary kick into ordinariness. But the ordinariness into which baptism kicks us need never be 'ordinary', or mundane, or lifeless, again; because I am marked by God's promise, marked for the purpose of living to the full. This is what it means to be 'marked for life' by the 'character' of baptism.

RE-MEMBERING BAPTISM: PAST EVENT, PRESENT REALITY

If the language of sacramental character was especially established through the systematic theologising and Christian philosophising of the medieval period, then it is through the tragic and blessed years of the sixteenth century, years of Reformation and Counter-Reformation, that we find a renewal of another way of speaking of the day-to-day-ness of baptism. For, typical of the Reformers, was a reassertion of the present reality of baptism, in ways which resonate deeply with the baptismal theology of St Paul. Baptism – far from being a past event, a rite of passage – is the mystery which strengthens the living of Christians, the profound reality of God's desire for us which can be called upon at all times.

Luther's perennial cry – a prayer of exclamation and strengthening – was 'I am baptised!' And this calling to mind the present power of the reality of his baptism was underpinned by a developed theology of 'baptismal piety',[27] in which what is tangible is the daily closeness of the Lord through the constant grace of baptism. As Luther writes himself: 'I am baptised, and through my baptism God, who cannot lie, has bound himself in covenant with me.'[28] Once again, we see that what is at the heart of the strenuous living of the Gospel in this man's life is a conviction about the reality of God's act upon him in baptism; a conviction which spills over into the realisation that if, indeed, God has done this in a human life, then the living of that life will be forever transformed and empowered.

This strong calling to mind of God's promise in baptism, this 're-membering' of the sacrament in daily life, is a source of wisdom and strength in the face of difficulty and sin. It is, above all, a call to hope. Precisely because the transformation of baptism is God's own work, we can be properly hopeful in the Lord, because we can put our trust in this divine work on us. For the Christian who remembers their baptism, that great blessing of knowing ourselves forgiven and absolutely loved is always to hand: 'As often as we fall, we must recall the remembrance of our Baptism and thus fortify our minds.'[29]

This tradition of the mystery of baptism as something upon which we are to call, in the here and now, is also reflected in the regular use of holy water in churches and homes in Orthodox and Roman Catholic traditions. The dish of holy water in my hall serves as just that kind of remembrance – going out into the world, and returning home, we go out as hearts promised to God and, more significantly, as hearts confident in the promise made us *by* God. Re-membering our baptism becomes the point of return and out-going. What is striking is that this 'memorial' sense of the living power of baptism – however we remember it – draws us into living lives with a rather oddly shaped view of time. As a people living baptism we are constantly naming in our present the saving 'past' and eternal event of Jesus' life, death and resurrection; and from this present recalling of 'the eternal past' we are called into a new sense of future, alive with hope and strength and promise. Living looks different from here.

BAPTISM: OFFICE AND MISSION AND ETHIC

What all this is beginning to make clear is the nature of baptism as a 'call' upon us, a vocation. The tradition, across 'the traditions', speaks in various ways of the abiding nature of baptism, and its implications for the way in which life is to be transformed for the Christian. Nor is this sense of things simply something of the past, something to be retrieved from a theological archaeological site, with painstaking and careful work, as if we were ignorant of the same mystery in our own time. For this everyday living of the sacrament is something attested to in the very life of those around us, and in our own living. At those places where grace is nurtured rather than cynicism and rejection; where the future is looked to in the Spirit of hope, rather than the wounds of the past given power; where the eternal promise and love of God in Christ is seen as what is real, rather than the various passing whims and idols of our lives – at these places the present livingness of baptism is made manifest and celebrated.

Within our contemporary Christian communities, too, there is a growing sense of the importance of renewing our sense of ourselves as a people whose only real vocation is to live baptism, in the variety of ways we are called to live it. Some 40 or so years ago the Second Vatican Council developed a potentially Church-transforming theology of ordinary lay life and vocation, based on its theology of baptism. In baptism, the Council teaches, the person becomes a member of Christ's body, and each shares fully, in particular ways, in Christ's mission and ministry.[30] It is baptism that so incorporates us into Christ himself, so that we participate in his three-fold offices of priest, prophet and sovereign. It is out of this baptismal sense that the Council Fathers are able to develop an understanding of ordinary living in the contemporary world, in terms of how we are to live as priests, prophets and members of Christ's royal household. As priests we are to 'consecrate the world to God', 'building up everything into Christ', constantly returning to and going out from the Eucharistic table.[31] As prophets we proclaim the good news about Jesus, and engage with our world of politics and human concern, always alive to the Word of God for which we are spokespeople, and sensitive to the things of faith.[32] As sharers in Christ's Kingship, we serve his coming Kingdom, and live lives shaped by that Christian paradox of the greatest being the least, of knowing power in weakness, of proclaiming the power of the crucified One.[33]

Here is a vivid and rich tapestry describing the life of the 'ordinary' Christian in the world, in terms which speak eloquently of the ways in which it is to be patterned by – configured to – Christ himself. Here is no comfortable rite of passage, or simple celebration of human life. Indeed, this goes far beyond even seeing in baptism God's love and salvation for all human beings. Here, that love of God is entered into *so as to transform the one loved* – the baptised – into a living, vibrant part of Christ's own life and mission. Baptism carries with it *office*. It is a gift and a call and a *task* (*munus*). In the words of a recent document of the Anglican Communion:

> Baptism gives Christians a vision of God's just order; it makes the Church a sign and instrument of the new world that God is establishing; it empowers Christians to strive for justice and peace within society.[34]

So we come to see more clearly that to live baptism is to participate in the Holy Spirit's transformation of the world – ourselves, our own ways of living, and the societies in which we live.

This brings us to something more, something deeper concerning the baptismal vocation. Here we begin to see that baptism is not simply about religious piety, about which group you belong to, or worship with. Baptism is not a private, devotional affair, but carries with it a *demand* for the transformation of life, and an empowerment to live in such a changed way. Baptism has, if you like, an ethical or political dimension – which is simply to say that baptism, in its living out by the baptised, *makes a difference to the world*, a difference oriented to God. It is this sense of 'baptismal ethic' which can enable the Methodist theologian James White to say:

> It is a contradiction of our baptism that we should have so many homeless and poor in our society, many of whom are baptised into us ... The deprivation of our neighbour is a sign

of our failure to take our baptism seriously. On the other hand, deeds of love and charity are a form of living out our baptism.[35]

To be baptised is to be called into the world to take up Christ's own mission. If we are baptised, we are ordained to this mission, commissioned to these ministries. And it is a call – even a claim upon us – to which we must respond in the very particular, concrete situations of our own lives.

CALL AND FORETASTE: ESCHATOLOGY AND PRESENTING THE FUTURE

There is a danger – especially in our own context – that all that has been drawn out from the long Christian tradition about the vocational nature of baptism will be simply translated into – 'Jesus is coming. Look busy!' We have established that baptism is not so much event, but rather something to be lived, got on with; the danger is that this will push us into that place of busyness which we so often understand our own lives to be. I'm sure I am not alone, for example, in hearing our baptismal vocation called upon as a reason why we should, as good Christian lay people, be volunteering for this or that church rota or ministry; here baptism has become a kind of provocation to activism, rather than a mysterious power for holiness and the transformation of life in imitation of Christ!

But then again, to speak of the 'ordinariness' of baptismal living might sound to some a giving up on the extraordinary and graced, in exchange for the mundane and burdensome – as if being baptised wasn't extraordinary! This couldn't be further from the truth of what is being spoken of here. What baptism does – and it is this that makes it extraordinary – is kick us out into our own ordinariness in the living power of extraordinary grace. We live ordinary lives full of grace, grace-fully.

To underscore this at the end of this chapter is simply to bring to the surface a thread which runs through the tradition, from Scripture into the reflections of our own time. Baptism points us to the future, and enables us to let go of the past which burdens us. Specifically, it orientates us to God's own future, his *eschaton*. This is the thread of 'eschatology' – the thinking about the last or 'end' things, the ultimate purposes of God, which are, of course, wholly mysterious to us.

Wholly mysterious, yes; but not, for that reason, entirely withheld from us, or closed to us. In baptism we come to *participate in* (which is not the same as 'fully understand'!) that hidden mystery of God which is, nonetheless, glimpsed, and lived out in our own time and space in the person of Jesus. By making us participate *in Jesus*, as risen and crucified, our baptism draws us, here and now, into that future which is God's own, into his own ends and purposes, 'which he set forth in Christ, as a plan for the fullness of time.'[36] Through the waters of baptism our past and future are transformed, as that radical forgiveness of God is known and embraced, and we move into a living by his promises, rather than by our own designs. It is in this way that our present – our ordinary, busy, mundane being to ourselves and the world – is continually transformed into a moment open to God's future.

This curious folding around of time about ourselves and our reality, so characteristic of Christian sacraments, is a theme found in one of Karl Rahner's sermons, preached on the occasion of a family baptism. In it we can see more clearly this 'present-ing' of God's future which is so much the hopeful living power of baptism as vocation:

> On this day we can see ourselves in this child ... and say to ourselves: 'You too began your life in this way. Did you continue so? Has the promise of this day been fulfilled in you? Has this day's sowing produced a harvest?' The day of our baptism returns to us out of our remote past. It has returned as our future – for blessedness or for judgement.[37]

The baptismal life is a life lived out of the hidden power of God's future, rather than out of the careful or strenuous planning of our own energies. The normal human anxieties of time – the pains and regrets of the past, the present efforts to get it right, the desperate need to control the unknowable future – all this is, in principle, transcended by baptism. After all, if we are baptised, we have already died with Christ, and live only in his new life of the resurrection. And so the past event of our baptism returns presently to us – in Scripture, in philosophical thinkings, in rememberings, in holy water stoops, and in liturgies – and always as our *future*, our call ahead into God. This is a living characterised by *trust*, strengthened by a power not our own and purposes we cannot plan for. We are a people led.

SOME CONCLUSIONS: NEW TIME, NEW PLACE, NEW LIFE

More than 30 years ago the Orthodox theologian Alexander Schmemann felt moved to lament in strong terms what he saw as the disappearance of baptism. He writes:

> ... to put it simply, baptism is absent from our life. It is, to be sure, still accepted by all as a self-evident necessity. It is not opposed, not even questioned. It is performed all the time in our Churches ... Yet, in spite of this, I dare to affirm, that in a very real sense it is absent, and this absence is at the root of many tragedies of the Church today.[38]

Here there is a profound sense of something essential to the life of the Church having been lost. It is, he argues, a loss to public liturgy, as the celebration of this sacrament becomes less and less a celebration of the whole congregation; because of this, it is a reality which has also lost its place in Christian piety, Christian ways of prayer and spiritual living. The tragic result is that 'baptism has lost its power to shape our Christian world view.'[39]

It is something of this same sense of loss that has been behind the concerns of this chapter. For Schmemann, it is a loss which sends him back to the liturgical texts of baptism, in keeping with his own Orthodox tradition, in order to reflect more deeply on what is found, proclaimed and celebrated there. In what follows a rather different path – perhaps a less straightforward one – shall be taken. What is called for is a new conversion, of thought and practice, to a baptismal way of living. Liturgy will have its part to play in forming us as a people of lived baptism; but it will also have its proper limits. In the end this is a conversion brought about by the Spirit, and we will want to hear it proclaimed through the diversity of Christian tradition, thinking and practice. We will, above all, need to hear it in our own hearts, and in our own ordinariness and every-day-ness. For it is here that baptism is to be lived.

PART TWO

BAPTISM FOR LIFE

CHAPTER FOUR

'IN THE NAME OF THE FATHER, AND OF THE SON, AND OF THE HOLY SPIRIT'

> *Go therefore and make disciples of all the nations, baptising them in the name of the Father and of the Son and of the Holy Spirit, and teaching them to obey everything that I have commanded you. And remember, I am with you always, to the end of the age.*
>
> Matthew 28:19–20, Jesus' final command to his followers

> *... I baptise you, in the name of the Father, and of the Son, and of the Holy Spirit.*
>
> The universal Christian formula at Baptism.[1]

> *Baptism is a gift of God, and is administered in the name of the Father, the Son, and the Holy Spirit.*
>
> WCC Faith & Order Paper 111, *Baptism, Eucharist and Ministry*, 'Baptism' article 1

Our very first observation about baptism brings us immediately up against the tension of the ordinary and the extraordinary with which we are already becoming familiar. To begin here, with the universally recognised Trinitarian words that must accompany Christian baptism, is to start in a difficult and surprising place. Yet, at first sight, it seems an oddly familiar place. At every baptism we will hear that the person is baptised 'in the name of the Father, and of the Son, and of the Holy Spirit'. For those of us from a Catholic Christian tradition, this formula also begins and ends our prayers, private and public. This naming of the Trinity persists even in our wider, 'post-Christian' culture, as a recognisable formula of Christianity. It's what Christians say about God. For all this familiarity, this wide use of this curious 'name', we remain largely cold towards the mystery about which we speak; and the mystery seems, all too often, pretty irrelevant to our lives.

It is this mystery of the Trinity, the name of God, Father, Son and Holy Spirit, which is at the heart of baptism. The words are routine – a formula. The danger is that the words can remain just that for us: *words*. Words which we can say, and even pray, without ever exercising too much thought over them. That's the trouble with ancient and universally accepted formulas; we begin, little by little, to miss the oddness of what is being said. We somehow allow such words to become so ritualistic, so much part of the culture of a religion, that we forget to *think* about them, and so we get out of the habit of letting thoughts be challenged by the starkness of these words. The formula becomes a way of taming the mystery. Human beings, after all, find things beyond them difficult to handle; we will generally prefer to make the mysterious, the transcendent, the plain difficult, easy and 'domesticated' and manageable. But, whether we're comfortable with it or not, there it stands: the Trinity is the inescapable, incomprehensible fact of Christian baptism.

In saying this, we can see for the first – but not the last – time, the complex ways in which reflecting on our baptism makes demands on us. In the very performance of baptism there is, set before our minds, something odd, apparently nonsensical, beyond normal powers of reasoning. Of course, we can choose simply to ignore it all as just too difficult. Or we can choose to respond to the call that this naming of the mystery of God makes upon us. For to name God in this way is to be called to think and pray and live more deeply in God's own life. This is what he reveals to us in Jesus; this is what he joins us to in baptism.

What follows are some reflections on what it might mean to respond to the mystery in this way.

DISCOVERING THE TRADITION

JESUS' BAPTISM AND THE REVELATION OF THE TRINITY

We will not find, on one level, a 'doctrine of the Trinity' set out for us in the New Testament – at least, we won't if what we mean by that is a systematic attempt to set down a reasoned statement of what it means to call on God as Father, Son and Spirit. But what we will find, at every turn, is God revealed in the life, death and resurrection of Jesus as Father, Son and Spirit. The narrative of the saving events of the Gospel depends on this: the virgin Mary becomes pregnant through the action of the Holy Spirit in her;[2] Jesus consistently addresses God as 'Father' in his prayers;[3] we hear the voice of the Father naming Jesus as his Son;[4] the Holy Spirit is not only the divine power in Jesus' ministry, but is also promised to his followers after his death as a lasting gift of communion between them and himself with the Father.[5] For the earliest Christians life was lived in the power of the Holy Spirit, sent to them at Pentecost. In this life they are children of God the Father, through the work of the Son. The Trinity shapes their living. Perhaps this is most vividly and eloquently put by St Paul in his letter to the Romans:

> For you did not receive a spirit of slavery to fall back into fear, but you have received a spirit of adoption. When we cry, 'Abba! Father!' it is that very Spirit bearing witness with our spirit that we are children of God, and if children, then heirs, heirs of God and joint heirs with Christ ...[6]

The Christian stands before God with Christ, and calls him 'Father' in the power of the Holy Spirit. Because we are joined to Christ, we are all 'first born sons'[7] like him, children of God, bearing the witness of the Holy Spirit within us. An extraordinary claim! This is a truth of Christian living which understands – somehow – that the mystery and oddness of God as Trinity, as three-and-one, enables us to share in divine life. God who is Father, Son and Spirit, is the God revealed in the saving work of Jesus, in his life and death, and in the Holy Spirit's communication of his risen life. The Christian story and its living is shaped by Trinity.

In all this scriptural witness to God as Father, Son and Spirit, one of the most outstanding images or stories is that of Jesus' own baptism by John:

> In those days Jesus came from Nazareth of Galilee and was baptised by John in the Jordan. And just as he was coming up out of the water, he saw the heavens torn apart and the Spirit descending like a dove on him. And a voice came from heaven, 'You are my Son, the Beloved; with you I am well pleased.' And the Spirit immediately drove him out into the wilderness ...[8]

Jesus' baptism cannot be seen in the same way as what we do as baptism today: his baptism pre-dates the saving mysteries of the cross and resurrection, which are the focus of Christian baptism, nor can there be any sense of Jesus' *needing* to be baptised for the forgiveness of sins.[9] But what we have in this story is a rich place for reflection on baptism and Trinity. For it is surely significant that it is in this baptism of Jesus that there is the most vivid image of the Trinity: the Son begins his ministry, making a formal act of turning to his call, and this leads to the voice of the Father being heard, revealing his love for the Son, as the Spirit comes down upon Jesus, anointing him for the work ahead. The turning point of baptism is, in Jesus' own life, the point at which God as Father, Son and Spirit is revealed.

From this point on, all that happens is carried out in the light of that baptismal revelation. As we have already seen, the Jesus we meet in the Gospels is the man who calls God 'Father', and who is uniquely empowered by the Holy Spirit. It is no coincidence, then, that immediately following the accounts of Jesus' baptism in the first three Gospels, we are told that the Holy Spirit 'drives' Jesus out into the wilderness. Here he is to be alone and totally dependent on his Father; here he is tempted and overcomes the devil, anticipating his final victory on the cross.

Reflecting and praying about this story in Jesus' life brings us closer to the living power of the Trinity, revealed in baptism. This is a memory of Jesus' life which can inform our thinking and faith in fresh ways: for here is no puzzling formula, not just something incomprehensible and too difficult to think about. Rather, here we have opened up before us a window into an act of God in the world, an act of power and transformation. And when we have this act described to us by those who saw it, what we see is God as Father, Son and Spirit. This is the God we name in our baptism, and in our recalling of baptism in our daily lives. This is God, who makes salvation a possibility for us in Christ's life, and in the abiding power of the Spirit.

In the end, Trinity reminds us, irreducibly, of the strange truth of Christian faith – that God, Creator of everything from nothing, loved us so much that he became a human being, like us. The story of Jesus' baptism, with its vivid revelation of Trinity, illustrates this. Jesus, a man living in a real historical and geographical context, takes on the same life and rituals as his neighbours, and is seen, in this solidarity with us, as God's Son, upon whom all the blessings and graces of heaven showered. It is Jesus as the human being in whom God is fully and perfectly present to the world and to human history, who opens this window onto the life of God, and makes it possible even for us to enter in, and share that life.

It is hardly surprising, then, that, in the history of the formulation of the Christian doctrine of the Trinity, it is actually theological meditation on Christ's divine humanity that calls up greater articulation of the doctrine of God as Trinity.[10] Central to our knowing God as Father, Son and Spirit, is the life and ministry, death and resurrection of Jesus – the Gospel. It is here that we know God as the God who shares our history, our place, our humanity, and who seeks us out only here, in our ordinary persons. It is here, too, that we encounter the depth of the mystery of being baptised into the divine life of the Triune God.

'IN THE NAME OF ...'

Being baptised 'in the name of the Father, Son and Holy Spirit' isn't simply a statement of belief about God; nor is it a mystical incantation. Remarkably, this doctrine or teaching about God carries with it a call to us – an invitation for us to be a part of that love between Father and Son, alive in the Spirit, sharing the life of God. This is what it means to be baptised 'in the name of' the God who is Trinity. Some thoughts on this phrase – 'in the name of' – can help us ponder this more.

This is, to us, an unusual phrase, to which we don't have much recourse ordinarily. The nearest we get to it in ordinary speech is in phrases such as 'in the name of the law', or in another legal reference – the idea that a transaction can be done 'in the name of' someone. But these odd terms are not a bad beginning for thinking about baptism: in different ways they give us an idea of an authority, a power by which something is said to happen. In a parallel way, it is by God's power and authority – specifically as he is revealed to us in the Gospel – that we are marked out in baptism. The name of God is, here, the naming of our salvation; and this is the power through which the mundane water-ritual of our liturgy becomes the saving act of God.

But there is more still. To speak of baptism 'in the name' seems to suggest, rather oddly, that a name can also be a place, somewhere we can be 'in'. A contemporary theologian ponders this in this way:

> This name is itself a very uncertain place, for how can one be situated inside a name unless it is a name one carries about wherever one goes? And in order to be inside a name, it must be an unusual name which opens up.[11]

As we shall see in this chapter, it is precisely because the name into which we are baptised is that of 'Father, Son and Holy Spirit', that it can function in this mysterious way. Here is a name which, by its very nature and truth, 'opens up' a new space for us to be. This name tells us of God, who reveals himself to us, and so is necessarily Trinity. Father, Son and Spirit, is how we encounter God in our world, meeting us in our space, and so making it his own place. This is 'God-for-us',[12] God who opens up the divine life and calls us into it, to share it with him.

So: doing this baptism thing 'in the name of' God means entering the space set out by God's revelation of himself, a space which is entirely under God's authority. To live under this name, and in this space, calls us to leave behind our own dislocated name and authority, in favour of life with and in God. To baptise 'in the name of' God, Father, Son and Spirit, is to place this life under the power and authority of this mystery. Nothing can ever be the same again, as all our actions and words become caught up in that mystery. In coming under that name we open ourselves to all the power, and blessings, and sufferings, and new life of Jesus' own life. Because of being 'in the name' we too may know ourselves driven out by the Spirit, crying to God as 'Abba!' in Gethsemane, and commissioned to serve the sick, the outcast, and the detested. In this name, too, will we hear the words of the Father, addressed to us: 'You are my beloved Son, in whom I am well pleased.'[13]

ONE NAME, OR THREE?

The Trinitarian formula itself points us to the heart of the mystery of the Trinity, and by its odd juxtaposition of words, calls us to think harder about what is being said, and the truth it is trying to express. To realise this requires simply that we look at what is being said afresh and recognise that it is grammatically and logically *non-*

sense. (It is also, and at the same time, of course, theo-logically, faith-fully *true*.) As Catherine Pickstock reflects, speaking of this formula:

> This is a difficult name. Whilst ordinary names are often multiple, they refer unambiguously to a particular person ... However, this name is a triple name, three different names which do not exactly name three differently named beings. The liturgical proceedings are not enacted 'in the names', for the three names are really only one name ...[14]

Right in front of us, in the baptismal formula, we have the traditional 'difficulty' of the Trinity presented. There is, even grammatically, both one name ('in the name of'), and three names ('the Father, and of the Son, and of the Holy Spirit'). The mystery spoken of here is a mystery of saying that God is *both* three *and* one – not three things very like each other, not three beings in close relationship, not one thing with three personas. No. The traditional doctrine of the Trinity asserts the simultaneous three-and-one-ness of God. And this is asserted in full awareness that it doesn't 'add up'.

So much in Christian life depends now on how we respond to this 'nonsensical' doctrine of God. There certainly have been and are people who understand themselves as Christian who would simply see in this incompatible statement of three and one an incoherence which must either be rejected, or modified until it makes sense. So, in the nineteenth century, we find the great Protestant theologian Friedrich Schleiermacher, calling on church people to revisit and review the doctrine of the Trinity, as it was clearly an incomprehensible (and so, it is argued, unhelpful) construct of the human mind.[15]

From the beginning until now there have always been those whose response to the doctrine of the Trinity is to revise it so that it is more comprehensible, more reasonable. Today the puzzle is often 'solved' by understanding the Trinity as a 'community'. Whilst the idea of God as both three *and at the same time* one hurts our heads to think of, and gives little that seems immediately edifying, the idea of God suggested by the Rublev icon as three people bound by hospitality, and inviting us in to share with them, is clearly more heartening, and less intellectually taxing.

What we need to ask in all this is, what is our motivation for making God's revelation of himself as Father, Son and Spirit easier to understand, or more 'helpful' to us? Are we, perhaps, in danger of wanting to settle *either* for the one *or* for the three in God, because it makes things more straightforward for us in so many ways? There is a danger that we will simply be attempting to make a God in our own image, to satisfy our own needs, and desires, and intellectual agendas. But the God who is three *and* one resists all such making of idols.[16]

We can be helped in receiving this difficult position of the one name which is three names by hearing some of the witnesses to this from the Christian tradition, both ancient and contemporary. The earliest Christians, among whom the formal doctrine of the Trinity was first worked out, knew that this was a teaching that didn't really make sense, and yet they delighted in such 'nonsense'. Only by this could the real truth of the mystery of God be expressed at all in human words. Most notably, the Cappadocian Fathers in the fourth century[17] bend the normal understanding of number in their discussion of Trinity. If we have to use number language, says Basil, we must do so 'reverently'; if we are to talk of 'three' and 'one', then these are not to be taken as 'numerical', as simply the sort of things you can count. That is not what this mystery of God is about, they tell us. And if this doesn't 'make sense' to you – well, why would you expect the revelation of Divinity to be within your intellectual grasp? Indeed, if you *could* understand God, he would hardly be 'God' in any true way, but rather an object of your own thinking.

These early Fathers of the Church could have responded to the revelation of God in the Gospel by trying to simplify, or rationalise; they were extremely well versed in philosophy, and able to think things through. The fact that they decided *not* to minimise the apparent nonsense of the Trinity, but rather, if anything, to celebrate it, tells us something about what it might be to respond to 'the name' which is three, in a way which doesn't seek simply to make sense, or make it 'meaningful' in our own terms. What these early Christians testify to is a living knowledge of God which allows the mystery simply to *be*. What we catch a glimpse of in all this, is the encounter with the God revealed at Jesus' baptism, which leaves the human person radically and intractably confronted with something beyond themselves – beyond their understanding, their sensible words, their cleverness of mind. This place of profound, wordless meeting is the point to which the 'nonsensical' words of the baptismal formula direct us.

If this all seems too worrying and obscure, we should remember that we are, after all, speaking about God. As the twentieth-century theologian Herbert McCabe points out, as Christians we should hardly be surprised if our language, in describing the truth God has shared with us, is, in the end, apparent 'nonsense'.[18] To imagine that, in my most truthful speech about God, I should make perfect sense, is to imagine that God himself can be summed up by human thoughts and words. In such a case, God would simply become another (albeit very important) object in *my* intellectual and verbal world. I would remain central, of course, and God would be understood by me. Naming God as One, and as Father, Son and Spirit in that very One-ness – to do this is to de-centre myself entirely, and become more and more mindful of the truth that God is *God*, and I am simply a creature (albeit one that is supremely and divinely loved – strangely!) in *his* world.

KNOWING THE UNKNOWABLE

There is much more, of course, that could be said about the Trinity as the power and name of baptism. Indeed, it is a first thought that will never leave us throughout our reflections on baptism, such is its uncompromising and permanent statement within the theology and performance of baptism. Once we begin to see – not without struggle – the living of baptismal life as a living thoroughly implicated in the mystery of the Trinity, just as Jesus' ministry, death and resurrection are – then nothing can be quite the same again. We live our lives in this nonsensical name of the God who loved us so much that he sent his Son to die for us,[19] and continues to fill our lives with his Spirit, empowering us, with Jesus, to call him 'Abba! Father!'[20] This living is only possible because the One God is Trinity.

If we can now begin to see the way in which being baptised in the name of the Trinity brings us, through Christ, into a new intimacy with God, such as is spoken of in Romans 8, then we might also have a sense of another, accompanying reality. This is a harder reality: such is the irreducible mystery of God that, even in coming to know God through his Trinitarian love and action for us, we come to know him (in the words of St Thomas Aquinas) as 'one unknown'.[21] Even as we are drawn into the love and divine life of Father, Son and Spirit, we find ourselves drawn to a place beyond understanding, beyond feeling, beyond our humanity. After all, *here* we find ourselves in the place where three *is* one, and one *is* three!

We are called, in the baptismal formula, to know God as one unknown. This can sometimes be a rather shocking thing to read. For us, here and now, knowing all about someone and understanding them is often used as a measure of friendship, of intimacy. These things surely accompany love. What this tradition of the unknowability of God tells us is that the very place where we encounter Love Itself, and know ourselves truly loved, is a place of un-knowing and mystery.

There is, it is worth remembering, a long and ancient tradition among Christians of a mystical silence, or wordlessness before God. This 'apophatic' or negative way ruthlessly recognises that, as creatures (and sinful ones at that), all we can ever say of God is flawed and inadequate. Radically, it must all be *negated*, as never fully true, if we are to see beyond the words and ideas *we* put together out of our own imagination, and be free to contemplate God as he himself chooses to reveal himself to us. We do, of course, have to say things; proclamation and communication are essential parts of the Christian vocation, and so the 'cataphatic' or positive works of theology and preaching and teaching are always necessary. But in order that we do not get seduced into thinking that our own words are themselves divine, the apophatic sense of their inadequacy before God is equally needed.

It is in this spirit that Denys the Areopagite, a theologian and mystic of the late fifth century, who exercised a huge influence over the development of the theological tradition, begins his *Mystical Theology* with a prayer. The prayer is addressed to Trinity, and speaks, with its impossible, non-sensical images of 'brilliant darkness' of the absolute transcendence of God, who, all the same, calls us, in his own power, into communion with him:

> Trinity!! Higher than any other being,
> any divinity, any goodness!
> Guide of Christians in the wisdom of heaven!

> Lead us up beyond unknowing and light,
> up to the farthest, highest peak of mystic scripture,
> where the mysteries of God's word lie simple,
> absolute and unchangeable,
> *in the brilliant darkness of a hidden silence* ...[22]

The Trinity draws us beyond our own reasoning; it is not a puzzle to be figured out.

The theologically proper 'nonsense' of God as three-and-one encapsulates this mystical tradition. In this incomprehensible naming of God we have both a positively expressed truth about God, in human words, and, in the apparent contradiction in terms, an inescapable and simultaneous undermining of what we are saying. It is only by remaining with this difficulty *as* difficulty, and not as a problem to be solved, that we can be sufficiently troubled to go on seeking out the unknowable God, who loves us. The impenetrable difficulty of this 'simple' formula beckons us into a place of wordless mystery, of mystical encounter with God. Paradoxically, it is in this place of unknowing that we come to know God as love, and as Father, Son and Spirit. We learn this not through our own efforts, but by surrendering these efforts to him, who alone is able to speak the truth about himself, and about ourselves.

All this, of course, points us firmly towards *prayer*.

LIVING THE MYSTERY

In this chapter so far, the words used and the ideas described have often borne an intolerable strain – how else could it be, when we set ourselves the task of exploring the truth about God in human words? But in struggling with these words we have caught glimpses, on the way, of what lies beyond the words. The deepening of our understanding of both the language, and the truth it seeks to express, can only happen through a profound living with these sometimes difficult and troubling things. What might it mean, in practice, to live a baptismal life 'in the name of the Father, and of the Son, and of the Hoy Spirit'? It is this that will concern us in these closing pages of this chapter.

Fundamentally, what all this points to is that the living of baptism is a living of mystery; and not just any mystery, but specifically the mystery of God's Trinitarian life, in which we are called to share. Being baptised can never be, then, simply a matter of having joined a particular group, for whom baptism is the way into the club; nor is it only a matter of adhering to a set of beliefs or stories. To say we are baptised in the name of the Trinity is to turn our whole living around to face the mystery of God, and say: This mystery, which I can't understand, and can hardly name in any sensible way – this is the most truthful, most real, most powerful and authoritative thing in my life.

When our daily lives are oriented to God's mystery in this way, all sorts of things begin to happen: our priorities are challenged, our sense of our cleverness is put in a new perspective; our self-importance is burst open for the insecurity it is. We learn, little by little, who we are, as creatures before God. And this happens through understanding the ways in which, through baptism in 'the name', we are thoroughly enmeshed in the story of redemption in Jesus, which is the story of the Trinity, as revealed to us. Bit by bit our sharing in the life of the Trinity, in all its mystery, makes more real in us Christ's own life, until with Paul we can say: 'it is no longer I who live but Christ who lives in me.'[23] We learn, through this being formed in the Trinity, to live Christ's life in the here and now – or rather, we learn to let him live that in us.

This finds all sorts of practical expression in our lives – both things we can decide to do, and other things that we will discover happening in and around us, by the power of the Spirit. For example, what we have discovered in the tradition about the insistence on the Trinity as mystery, suggests that the baptised person is called to become someone more and more at home with mystery. When you think about it, that's rather disturbing; for human nature recoils from what it cannot control, or understand, or dismiss, and it is disturbing – 'vertiginous' almost! – to spend more and more of our lives on the edge of something we cannot understand. We can only even think about doing it because we know that, central to the story of the Trinity which is the Gospel, is the fact that God loves us; and love casts out fear.[24]

Living alongside mystery forms us in a certain security, or courage, stemming from trust in God. The 'nonsense' of the name of the Trinity is simple silliness without faith in God's Word. He has given his Word, and it is all we have to go on, and all we need, in the end. Such dependence on God, and trust in his care for us, draws even our most ordinary living into an end, or future, which is beyond the everyday and mundane. Whatever the fearful and fearsome situation into which we go, we know that God is bigger than all that, and that our end is in him.

There is an ethical reality here, too. The baptised person's repeated gazing into God forms eyes and heart in ways which enable us to gaze into the mysteries of human suffering, sin, and brokenness with a new sense of what is most real in all this: God, and his love for us. The man or woman who allows the name of the Trinity to be the place they inhabit, accepting the intractable mystery, and not seeking to rationalise it – this is a person who is likely to recognise that the true and the good isn't *always* distinguished by the best or clearest arguments, and that much that is graced and holy in a life cannot be summed up in thoughts and words. Living 'in the name of the Father, Son and Spirit' calls us into the places of human need and achievement with a fresh perspective, and a new source of wisdom. The Trinity as the name we inhabit makes a difference in our lives.

How are we to bring this sense of 'living in the name' into our everyday lives? Ultimately we each need to let the mystery itself into our thinking and praying, and it will lead us into the ways where we can most fully live that life. But some practical suggestions can be made.

MEETING THE MYSTERY IN SCRIPTURE

In deepening our living sense of the mystery of God, there can be no substitute for allowing the Word of God in Scripture to speak to us. This requires, on our part, discipline and the deliberate making of time and space, and an attentive thoughtfulness for reading and dwelling on (and in) these words. In all the chapters that follow, our first practical suggestion for nurturing the living of baptism will be to refer to the praying of certain Bible passages. The suggestion is to allow a good, long, awake piece of time – say half an hour or more – for the quiet, repetitive reading of a passage. The ancient tradition of reading a passage slowly aloud, first, and then taking time to look through each phrase thoughtfully, is envisaged. And where a word, or phrase, or image strikes us, we stop, and 'pondering these things in our hearts',[25] allow our thoughts to grow in prayer towards God who is, we can be sure, seeking to speak with us.

In seeking to grow in our sense of the Trinity as the mysterious, yet present, heart of Christian living, the following passages might be especially helpful:

- The baptism of the Lord: Matthew 3:13–17; Mark 1:1–13.
- Jesus coming to humanity as an act of Trinity: Luke 1:26–38.
- The call to share in the life of Trinity: John 14:15–26.
- The Christian's participation in Trinity: Romans 8:9–17.

ACTIONS TO EMBODY THE MYSTERY

The Gospel narratives, and the words of others, and our thoughts are important ways into deepening our sense of Trinitarian-shaped living. But it can never be just about words, especially given what we have said about the radical-ness of the mystery of God. There are, also, simple practices of Christian tradition which form us by their habitual reference to the mystery we ponder. Here are some of them:

- *The custom of crossing yourself with holy water as a reminder of baptism.* A tradition more familiar to Catholic and Orthodox parts of the Christian community, this simple act can become part of the practice of Trinity and baptism in our homes. The presence of holy water bowls at front doors can easily be adopted – and adapted – so as to become a powerful reminder both of baptism, and of Trinity, as we sign ourselves 'in the name of the Father, and of the Son, and of the Holy Spirit'. This is a habit of repetitive prayer which, at its best, marks all our comings and goings with the remembrance of our baptism, and 'the name' in and under which we live.
- *Using the 'Glory be'.* Traditional hymns usually conclude with a verse giving praise to the Trinity, reflecting the ancient custom, still used in the Catholic reciting of the Office, of concluding the praying of the psalms with the 'Glory be'. 'Glory be to the Father, and to the Son, and to the Holy Spirit; as it was in the beginning, is now, and ever shall be, world without end. Amen.' This simple and short prayer draws us easily into the

eternal and present mystery of Trinity, and reminds us of our call to share in this life.

OPENING OURSELVES TO THE MYSTERY IN PRAYER

A major part of this chapter's reflection on Trinity has been to remind ourselves of the profound mystery of God – a mystery which is not tamed by our words and formulae, but rather confronts us in the very 'nonsense' of the words themselves. The call to live on the edge of this mystery is a call, in some way, to *contemplation*. We are so used to prayer and worship as things we do, words we say, songs we sing, that we are in danger of losing touch with that long tradition of silent, empty prayer, which is essential for our growing in knowledge of God 'as one unknown'. The living of baptism as life 'in the name of' the Trinity needs to find time where the mind, body and heart of the baptised person can simply be *emptied* before God. This silent, wordless and thought-less being with God isn't always or often a pleasant or stimulating experience, as the mystic saints of the Christian tradition bear witness![26] But that is not its purpose. Rather, this is time and presence given simply to God, for its own sake. Its practice draws us into that reality of God which it is so easy for us to ignore and avoid (because we really do want to avoid it, on the whole!) in our day-to-day living. It is, though, what makes it possible for the ordinariness of life to be broken open to the extraordinariness of baptism – the absolute extraordinariness of the divine life of the Trinity.

EVERYDAY WITNESS TO THE MYSTERY

It would be a mistake, in the light of all this, to imagine that life in the Trinity, the living of baptism 'in the name', was simply a matter of devotion and personal piety. What these practices of deepening our sense of the truth of God do is change our sense of the world around us and – bit by bit – our relationships, priorities, sensitivities and tastes are transformed, configured to Christ. The details of how this might happen are too particular to each person to be specified here; but some questions to ourselves as baptised, Trinity-shaped people might help draw out the consequences of our mysterious, Trinitarian-lived faith:

- If I live in the mystery of the name of God, how does that challenge my expectations of what is 'reasonable', 'convincing', of what 'makes sense'? What are my criteria for discernment and judgement of truth? Do I discern truth according to what makes sense to me, or according to some criterion beyond myself?
- Given the mystery that is named by Father, Son and Spirit, how much reverence do I give, in my own speech, in talking about and using that language of God? How do I respond to careless or wrong or blasphemous uses of God's name? Do I watch my words, in ways that make them more likely to be able to disclose something of God's mystery?
- How might these reflections on God as Trinity challenge my priorities, my sense of what is most real? Is my major area of concern the material, the here and now? Or is there a way in which God's reality breaks through, practically, into the way I plan my days?

To live baptism, is to live life 'in the name of the Father, and of the Son, and of the Holy Spirit'. It is to live, primarily, in the mystery of God's reality. If we do this, we will live differently – marked out by the story of God's saving love for all human beings. We will become witnesses to what is, in fact, most real for men and women – the life of divine love which God has called us to.

CHAPTER FIVE

BAPTISM AS THE TOMB: SHARING IN CHRIST'S DEATH

Do you not know that all of us who have been baptised into Christ Jesus were baptised into his death? Therefore we have been buried with him by baptism into death ... Romans 6:3–4

Christ, by baptism, has made us partakers of his death, engrafting us into it ... John Calvin, Institutes, IV. 15, 5

We ask you, Father, with your Son, to send the Holy Spirit upon the waters of this font. May all who are buried with Christ in the death of baptism, rise also with him to newness of life.

Prayer for the Blessing of the Water,
Roman Rite of the Christian Initiation of Adults

In a culture which more normally associates baptism with the birth of children, and the celebrations of that new, just-beginning life, it jars a bit to be reminded of *death* in the middle of it all. Such is the joy of our baptismal celebrations, and the natural happiness which particularly surrounds the infant being baptised, and the grateful and rejoicing parents, that it can come as a bit of a shock to have the theme of death pointed out. And yet, there it is: in our baptismal liturgies, and – from the earliest times – in the scriptural understandings of baptism.

So it is for St Paul, offering one of the earliest reflections on baptism. For Paul, being baptised means precisely sharing in that extraordinary saving tragedy which is Christ's death on the cross. This sense of his baptism as making him a true sharer in Christ's death emerges as a key feature of Paul's own theology and personal vocation. He is able to state, quite boldly, 'I have been crucified with Christ', and, because of this baptismal sharing, 'it is no longer I who live, but Christ who lives in me.'[1] We remember, too, how Jesus uses the language of baptism to refer to his suffering and death.[2] Baptism is, from the beginning, seen as a real kind or type of dying with Christ. Baptism is about the cross. Our living of baptism needs, too, to be 'cruciform', cross-shaped.

It was – as is often the case! – a comment from my (then eight-year-old) daughter that exposed to me the challenge of this part of the baptismal tradition. Whilst talking to her, in preparation for her receiving the Eucharist for the first time, we started discussing baptism and what it meant to be baptised. In a scripturally purist spirit, I made reference to the way in which baptism makes us participate in Christ's death. It is, I confidently asserted, as if, when a baby is baptised in the font, we bury him or her in Jesus' death. Baptism is a kind of dying, so that we can be with Jesus in his new life. She looked at me, with a penetrating, slightly disgusted look – 'Well! That's not very nice.' And, of course, it's not.

I think Alice got over this rather clumsy bit of parental catechesis; but I'm not sure I did. Her natural, healthy consternation at the theologically and biblically sound idea that baptism calls us to a kind of dying, is something which has persisted in my own thinking and prayer both as a gift, and as a trouble. In a simple, immediate way, the conversation I've recalled raises many questions. And the central question is, what on earth might it mean faithfully to live our baptisms as a dying with Christ? This is a hard question; it directs our gaze to places where we would rather not look. Which is, I suppose, why, in fact, we so often keep our heads down, and seek to forget this part of our Christian tradition. For, in this universal and most ancient understanding of baptism, we find themes of death, sacrifice, suffering, and loss; and these are the very things that challenge a great deal of the healthy and happy living which we struggle to maintain. In a context where we are raised to believe that self-fulfilment, material well-being, health, and comfort are self-evident goods (and I'm not denying that they might be good), and in which death and sacrifice are things that appal, and are often to be hidden, avoided – in such an environment the call to examine our baptismal living as a kind of real dying is bound to be troublesome.

Troublesome, yes. But also true and blessed in ways which can, perhaps, truly serve life in such an apparently life-affirming and yet death-dealing culture as our own. The truth is that baptism reminds us of the way in which death is at the centre of the Christian message – not as the last word, to be sure, but certainly as an essential part of the drama of salvation. As such, the cross, and Christ's dying, becomes a central part of our saved living as baptised people. Baptism calls into question our 'normal' sense of life and death. The Lutheran theologian, Wolfhart Pannenberg, puts this well and challengingly when he writes:

> ... the future death of the baptised one is anticipated in the act of baptism ... The future death of the person, and therefore his or her entire life history is anticipated in the rite of baptism, in order to be implanted into the person of Jesus Christ, into His cross and resurrection.[3]

Baptism, like Eucharist, reminds us forcefully of the risen life of Jesus which is the divine response to his self-sacrificing death. In doing this, baptism (like Eucharist) not only proclaims to us the victory over death, but calls us to look again at how we live our lives, inevitably directed in time towards our own death. We can do this, and carry the reality of our own inevitable dying with us, in the abiding knowledge of Christ's own saving death, and ultimate victory over death. The baptismal vocation is, on one level, a call into the tomb. But it is also a call to discover in our own tomb, in our own sure end in death, something surprising, something of God. Only if we are bold enough and graced enough to go there, will we see death – and life – in a way renewed by Christ.

This is a hard message, perhaps, and maybe at first sight it is a rather gloomy one. But deeper reflection on baptism as a sharing in Christ's death can not only open up a new kind of joy to us, but it can also transform the real gloom of death which – if we are honest – does inevitably encroach on human living in this world. The following reflections will try to open up what is meant by this, by looking first at the Christian tradition regarding the death of Christ on the cross, and then exploring some of its implications for baptismal living.

EXPLORING THE TRADITION

'NOTHING BUT CHRIST, AND HIM CRUCIFIED'

When St Paul writes what we know as his first letter to the Corinthian Christians, he is clearly addressing a rather troubled and fractious group of people. These people clearly need, he feels, to be reminded forcefully of the heart of his preaching of the Gospel among them. So, right at the start of this letter, Paul points out to his readers that, when he was among them, he preached nothing wise or clever, but 'only Jesus Christ, and him crucified'.[4] Paul confronts our supposed cleverness and wisdom with the cross – 'the folly of God' – which is wiser than all our own cleverness. This is the wisdom of God, which looks like foolishness to us: Christ crucified – a tortured, stripped form of a man, hanging dead on a cruel instrument of execution.[5] This is, says Paul, all he preached; this is what our Christian baptism refers us to.

This early proclamation of the 'good news' that we find in St Paul's letters is entirely in keeping with what we see in St Mark's Gospel. Significantly, this Gospel is generally recognised by scholars as the earliest of the Gospels; its pared-down narrative has been commonly described as 'a Passion narrative with a long introduction'. Such a description makes clear that the earliest attempt to write down what had happened in Jesus' life and work was most concerned with focusing on the suffering and death – or 'the Passion' – of Jesus. Mark's narrative compels us, with urgency, towards this story of suffering and death. Indeed, it is even debatable as to whether he originally included the account of the resurrection which we now have at the end of this Gospel.[6] For the author of Mark's Gospel, as for Paul, the point of Jesus' life, work and teaching is to be found in some pre-eminent way in his suffering and death. It is the cross that is seen as the culmination of Jesus' ministry.

It is a hard, demanding task to reflect on the accounts of Christ's suffering and death that we receive in the biblical tradition. This is a story of the deepest human fear and anxiety,[7] the appalling betrayal by a friend through an act of affection,[8] loneliness and the uselessness of those closest and most loved,[9] and unspeakable physical degradation, pain and humiliation. This is a story about the full human horror of death. Simply on that human level we are moved, and repelled, and outraged. And then there is the realisation of faith: that all this is focused on Jesus – the healer, and teacher, and Son of God. It is the Lord of Life who is slain; the King of Love who is betrayed and rejected. It is this story of suffering and cruelty that the Christian tradition claims as the story of human salvation.

The idea that Christian discipleship – the living of baptism – is bound up in the mystery and horror of the cross is present in the Gospel narratives themselves. We can see this in Mark's Gospel. Here, there is a turn in the narrative around chapter 9, after which the momentum towards the Passion narrative is keenly felt. Just before this, at the end of chapter 8, Peter names Jesus as 'the Messiah', God's anointed one. Whilst accepting this response from Peter, Jesus none the less immediately puts this title of Messiah in a new context, as he begins to teach his disciples that he must be rejected, suffer and die.[10] Peter's reaction to this is to rebuke Jesus, who, in his turn, argues with Peter, saying that he cannot see things the way God does. It is from this difficult exchange of friends that we have Jesus' description of the life of Christian discipleship as one of bearing the cross: 'If anyone wants to become my follower, let him deny himself and take up his cross and follow me.'[11] Following Jesus, at this turning point towards suffering and death, is clearly described as a sharing in that journey. If the cross on Calvary is the culmination of Jesus' ministry, it is also the shape that must be given to day-to-day discipleship.

This strong language of cross-burdened living is paralleled in Luke's and Matthew's Gospels[12] and has its resonance, too, in the Fourth Gospel (according to John). In John's account of the Last Supper, Jesus' departing command is to *love one another*; and this command is epitomised by 'laying down one's life for one's friends'.[13] In the same Gospel, Peter's own ministry of tending and nourishing Christ's people is cast in terms of his dying.[14] What is clear is that the rather nice-sounding command to *love* is, also, a command to 'lose your life' and to 'deny yourself'; it is a command to share in Christ's death.

BUT WHY THE CROSS?

Whilst the testimony of Scripture to the real central significance of the cross to our salvation is consistent and clear, there is little in the New Testament itself to help us answer questions of why, or how this 'works'. The Gospels, as we have seen, see Christ's suffering and death as essential to his work; and so, too, something like this is to be found at the heart of the following of Jesus by the true disciple. For St Paul the crucifixion is presented as the necessary, unquestionable heart of the Gospel proclamation: it is through the cross that the Father 'reconciles to himself all things';[15] it is because Christ died 'for us' that we can know ourselves as 'justified by his blood'.[16] These are the traditional terms in which Christianity has spoken of being saved by Christ's death; they are scriptural, and lie at the heart of the original proclamation of the good news. Christians of varying kinds, and of various levels of involvement in the Church, will be familiar with these frankly odd terms through the singing of popular hymns. Whether the traditional, 'When I survey the wondrous cross', or the more contemporary, 'Shine, Jesus, shine', the language of being 'redeemed' by the cross persists. As is often the way, the combination of real difficulty and over-familiarity seems to me to have prevented us hearing afresh, and with renewed understanding, what is being said here.

Part of the problem is that the scriptural evidence, as we have seen, is at once both perfectly consistent about Christ's dying as a central and essential part of his saving work, and, at the same time, pretty much lacking in any *explanation* as to why or how this should be. To be sure, there is a plethora of images used to describe what is going on at the crucifixion: Jesus is seen as overcoming the oppressive powers and authorities of the cosmos, which hold humanity ever accountable for what is wrong in the world, 'nailing it to the cross';[17] Christ might be seen as paying the price, or making satisfaction for human sin;[18] or the cross might be seen as an example to us, to inspire us to right living.[19] All these, and other, images are in Scripture, and, human beings being what they are, they have each, at one time or another, been taken out from their scriptural context, and systematised so as to 'make sense' of the cross. So we have seen God the Father portrayed as a wrathful God demanding the price of the Son's death; or the Son standing as judged in some kind of cosmic courtroom on our behalf.[20] All these extended metaphors fail, in the end, for one reason or another to speak of the mystery of faith in the cross. None of it quite seems to add up.

In the end, perhaps, what the cross speaks of most eloquently, and real-ly, is the sheer *humanity* of God in Jesus. Perhaps our inevitable death, and our ability to know about it, to contemplate it, to dread it – perhaps it is this which is one of the most powerful and decisive facts of our humanity. It is this which keenly defines 'the human condition'. We know, even as we celebrate life, and the birth of new people, that death is where we're all headed. It is not for nothing that the ancient Greek philosopher Plato taught what he had learnt from Socrates: that the purpose of philosophy was to prepare one for a good death.

But Jesus' death is about more than learning something from him – though it might be that as well. The Christian tradition, rooted in Scripture, is clear that Jesus' death *makes a difference*. In particular, the cross of Christ transforms the relationship between God and humanity. For here on the cross, above all, we see God's loving solidarity with us, at the point of death – the boundary point of our human knowing and consciousness. As the Dominican theologian Herbert McCabe writes:

> ... Jesus died of being human. More than that: all humans die, but he was so human he had to be killed.[21]

When the perfect, sinless humanity which is God's humanity in Jesus comes into a rather messed-up world, full of competition, anxiety, jealousy and power struggle – well, it is hardly surprising that this man, who is God, ends up not just dying, but being rejected, humiliated, tortured, and murdered. Herbert McCabe again:

> There is a twist or a contradiction in our human life that means we build a world unfit for humans. The only way to get by in it is to restrict your humanity rather carefully, otherwise you will get hurt ... You have to ration your love, keep a wary eye out for enemies, if you want to survive. Now Jesus did not ration his love, so naturally he didn't last.[22]

Jesus goes to the cross for being completely human, for never rationing his love. To live baptism is to live called into such reckless loving, without minding the consequences. To live baptism means growing more and more human, in ways that brings us hard up against suffering and death. This is what denying yourself, and taking up the cross daily must be about. And it's OK; because, in Jesus, God has done it all ahead of us, and continues, through our baptism, to do it all in us.

For all our intellectual struggling with this mystery of the cross – the wisdom of God, the folly of men[23] – it remains a gift to us. In it our greatest human fear, and sufferings, find their place in God, in the eternal life and love of the Trinity. What we know in the cross is that, in Jesus, God walks the path of deepest human pain and loss. He is even to be heard at the last point of despair that attends human mortality: 'My God, My God! Why have you forsaken me?'[24] There is no place in human experience he cannot go – and, unlike us, he goes there in love and freedom and without any sin or wrong in him. Baptism joins us to this place – the cross – where divine love reaches into the depths of human depravity, and goes on loving to the end (and, in the end, living).

'MAKE ME KNOW THE SHORTNESS OF MY LIFE, THAT I MAY GAIN WISDOM OF HEART'

It is worth, perhaps, spending a little time at this point really facing the difficulty of what is being spoken of here – the difficulty of our own mortality, that fact of life which we spend most of our life denying in some way or another: we are all born to die.

We are, understandably, not easy around this kind of thinking. However 'strong' our faith, death is, quite properly, horrible to us. As Pope John Paul II lived his last few days and hours as so public a witness to Christian hope and the suffering of the cross, I was reminded of his words of some 20 years previously. Death, he writes,

> ... is often awaited even as a liberation from the sufferings of this life. At the same time, it is not possible to ignore the fact that it constitutes as it were a definitive summing-up of the destructive work both in the bodily organism and in the psyche ... death primarily involves the dissolution of the

> entire psychophysical personality of man ... the evil which the human being experiences in death has a definitive and total character.[25]

Here is no romanticised picture of the immortal soul somehow floating away out of the body into a bright new life. Resurrection faith is, to be sure, what frames this papal letter; but it is also what makes the real destructiveness of death as a total letting go of all that we are, important and honestly central.

The witness of many saints alerts us to the real and proper horror of death; and with that witness comes, too, a thorough and deepened sense of the importance of Christ's own suffering and dying for our being able to share in his life. It is in communion with Christ's own suffering and death that the saints are able to walk the path of their own frailty and mortality in ways which continue to give glory to God, and speak the truth of his love for the world. We need only think of the agonising last months of Therese Martin (St Therese of Lisieux) to catch a glimpse of this.[26]

Death, even of the saints, is just horrible. But given Jesus' death, that's hardly to be wondered at.

Now there is a way of taking all this on which is morbid and unhealthy. This is *not* what the baptismal sharing in Christ's own death is meant to be. Rather, baptism into the tomb of Christ frees us, on a deep level, in relation to our own mortality. In this knowing of our own death in Christ's death our inevitable mortality can become the place of wisdom, and life, and love – whilst remaining, for most of us, properly fearful. In baptism, in some mysterious way, we have *already died* with Christ, and live with a new life. We are free to live open to God's future for us, because everything we might think of accomplishing, is already accomplished in Christ. All we need do is live in him, and know our life – and our death – as his.

THE CROSS AND CHRISTIAN DISCIPLESHIP

This is hard for us to take. Indeed, it's never been easy for men and women to hear and live this call to the cross. But for all that, the Christian tradition is full of witness to this laying down of life which is love. In different, myriad ways, the faithful living of baptism has marked the story of the Church with an endless stream of 'witnesses' – in the Greek, *martyroi*, martyrs – who through day-to-day loving, through heroic suffering, or public martyrdom, proclaim the truth that, in baptism, we have been buried with Christ.[27] We are free to live lives without huge ambition, or burdensome plans for our own satisfaction, but simply – riskily! – patterned by an increasingly non-rationed loving, leading to Christ's cross, and new life.

From time to time I visit a Carmel – a strictly enclosed community of women religious – where day-to-day life is built around a discipline of frequent common prayer, household chores, and short times of recreation. I have, over the years, read about 'Carmelite spirituality'; I know a bit about the rise of monasticism, the thinking behind enclosure and solitude, expressed in the Desert Fathers, or the Carthusian tradition, as well as Carmel. It is, in its way, starkly attractive for its purity of intention, its radical living of the life of prayer before God. But it is only by spending time trying to share a bit of the life of the Carmel that I have come to realise something very challenging about this prayerful, simple life. It hit me hard one visit, during yet another saying of the Divine Office – an event which comes around with tedious regularity! The point was this: commitment to the life of Carmel means – at least in some sense – being prepared to spend your life waiting to die.

I didn't like the idea; it is altogether too challenging for a generally cheerful, worldly lay woman, looking forward to the next exciting, or tasty, or pleasurable thing. Yet when the community generously welcomed me into their enclosed garden, and showed me – among more ordinary, beautifully horticultural and growing things – the little cemetery where they all intend to end up, there was a simple humour about it which was, without doubt, a grace. Spending your life in prayer and simple living, so as to be able to die in Christ – well, there is something here of an important witness to the rest of us. In a way, what is shocking about it is how it tells us the truth about our own *apparently* more exciting, more ambitious living; it, too, is a preliminary to dying. The Carmel speaks to us nakedly of the call of baptism.

This experience – so keenly and painfully felt – reminded me too that, in its origins, baptism was always closely associated with the shortness of life: not 'just symbolically', not simply in terms of a theology or spirituality, but materially and historically in the risking of life through becoming part of Christ's body, the Church. In the early Church, during the periods of persecution, becoming a Christian, being baptised, was sharply about putting your life on the line. So Ignatius, writing very early in the second century, is able to understand his Christian discipleship, and looming death, in terms of Christ's cross.[28] Indeed, the language he uses to describe his martyrdom is profoundly sacramental, referring not only to baptism, but to Eucharist as well: he sees himself as poured out on an altar, like sacrifice;[29] consumed by wild beasts, he sees himself as ground into flour in order to become Christ's pure bread;[30] his dying for Christ is the culmination of his birth into Christ's life:

> ... so far as I am concerned, to die in Jesus Christ is better than to be monarch of earth's widest bounds. He who died for us is all I seek; He who rose again for us is my whole desire. The pangs of birth are upon me; have patience with me, my brothers, and do not shut me out from life [i.e., do not try to prevent Ignatius' death], do not wish me to be stillborn. Here is one who only longs to be God's; do not make a present of him to the world again ... Leave me to imitate the Passion of my God.[31]

For Ignatius it is only this dying in Christ which will make him 'truly human';[32] his devotion to Christ who was crucified is such that he can 'yearn for death with all the passion of a lover'.[33] Yet, in all this, there is a proper human fear, and anxiety about the sufferings that face Ignatius. This is not a morbid, suicidal or masochistic sense. Rather, it is the voice of one who, in Christ, knows that his own life, and death, and eternal happiness has already been accomplished – should he choose to participate in it.

Few of us, in our own context, face this kind of martyrdom, though we should be mindful that there are places in the world where baptism still means the threat of torture, imprisonment and death. Yet, in our relative security, living in tolerant, liberal societies, the theology of baptism still calls us to recognise our vocation to the cross. We are still summoned to the daily taking up of our cross, the laying down of life, which is Christian love, the denying of self, and the absolute refusal to ration loving, however much this brings suffering. These things bind all the baptised, as people 'buried with Christ', across all contexts and ages.

Sometimes baptism leads people through persecution and violent death. But the tradition also knows that at other times, perhaps as painfully, the same baptismal calling leads us into a transformed way of living each day. It is this kind of daily 'martyrdom of love' that St Jane Frances de Chantal speaks of:

> What happens [in this kind of living martyrdom] is that love seeks out the most intimate and secret place of your soul, as with a sharp sword, and cuts you off even from your own self ... I do not think that the martyrdom of love is less painful than the other [of death], because 'love is as strong as death', and martyrs of love suffer infinitely more by staying alive to do God's will than if they had to give up a thousand lives for their faith and love and loyalty.[34]

It is something like this martyrdom of love, this daily giving up of life, that we are called to in living baptism.

LIVING THE MYSTERY

There is, in this testimony of the Christian tradition, a rather stark challenge, that can seem so big, so demanding as to be hopelessly overwhelming. I, for one, cannot (yet!) share Ignatius' yearning for death; nor, despite my joyful visits to the Carmel, do I feel able (or called) to embrace a monastic style of living in all its discipline and routine. Even Jane Frances de Chantal's living martyrdom of love sounds unpleasantly painful. This is a part of living baptism which seems especially alien to all we understand about being 'healthy and happy' in our own culture.

Still, this long, consistent tradition can hardly be ignored. I suspect the truth of it in our own lives can only become real when we are honest about our own distaste for such cruciform living, and open our hearts and time and minds to the power of Christ *in us*. For we must remember that the call of baptism is also a *power*, a grace and gift, by which, at the deepest level of reality ('ontology', our very being), we have a share in Christ's person, his life, death and resurrection. We must be clear: none of this is possible as a sheer act of human will. Indeed, it really wouldn't be healthy for this to be imposed on our lives, by ourselves or anyone else. St Jane Frances affirms this, asserting that the martyrdom of love can only be freely responded to – 'he [God] never forces our free will.'[35] No. Living the cross is *only* possible, and joyful, and life-giving in the realisation of the truth that 'it is not I who live, but Christ in me.'[36] It is by the power of Christ at work in us, that the Lord is able 'to accomplish abundantly far more than all we can ask or imagine.'[37] What we need to learn, more and more, is how to open up our lives – our living – to that cross-defined loving of the baptismal vocation.

SHAPING OUR THINKING THROUGH SCRIPTURE

Taking up the idea of reflecting and praying on Scripture as an essential part of the formation of baptismal living (see above, pp. 53–4), here are some suggestions for reflecting on the cross, and how it shapes our lives.

Perhaps the most powerful scriptural passages are those which describe the story of the Passion and death of Christ. They are long, and may need to be read over some days, or slowly, with a good chunk of time given over to the story, allowing it space to be heard. Reading one of these narratives aloud can sometimes enable us to hear and notice things which we've not realised before. Prefacing such reading with a prayer, asking that the Spirit will guide our thinking and hearing, and draw us into the mystery of the cross, is an important help in this.

- The Passion according to Mark: chapters 14—15.
- The Passion according to Matthew: chapters 26—8.
- The Passion according to Luke: chapters 22—3.
- The Passion according to John: chapters 18—19.

Then there are passages which speak vividly of how Christian discipleship shares in Christ's suffering and cross:

- Matthew 10:34–9.
- Mark 8:31–6.
- Mark 10:35–45.

And St Paul's vivid sense of the cross as defining his own calling and work:

- Romans 6:3–11.
- 1 Corinthians 1:17–31.
- Galatians 2:19–20.

SIGNS AND SYMBOLS

The Christian tradition has always recognised that 'ordinary living' does not always lend itself to long periods of prayer or reading. Important, and, in the end, necessary as these are, there are periods in our lives when we have to 'snatch' at moments, times when we just need to find ways of quickly, and routinely, touching the beautiful things of our faith. Just as there are times in a marriage when work and pressures of raising a family mean that the couple might only manage a few minutes of conversation every now and then, and a brief kiss goodbye or hello – so, too, there are periods of 'routine loving' in our faith. That's normal, and OK, and provision is made for it in all sorts of ways.

One of the things that can be useful for this habitual or routine reflection on the cross is images – crosses or crucifixes hung on walls, or on the bedside table, or close to our hearts around our necks. Coming from a tradition where it is the crucifix that is more usual, with its tortured figure of the dead Christ hanging from the cross, I am perennially shocked by this public 'decoration' of home and body with such a (humanly) appalling image: it's like wearing a gallows as a piece of jewellery, or having an image of a victim of torture of your wall. It is, let us be truthful, shocking, to be about your business, making the bed, or rushing out the door to school, and catch a glimpse of such a thing.

But it is right and proper that this shock finds its place in our lives. Its power to call us back, immediately and briefly, to the mystery that the larger part of this chapter has been describing is attested to through the ages. It may be that a renewed sense of this imagery as an habitual part of our domestic living can act as a reminder of our baptismal vocation, when we are in the very thick of its muddle and practical demands.

Another less cerebral, more embodied remembering of our call to the cross, again more familiar to Catholic Christian traditions, is the *via crucis*, the way of the cross. This ancient tradition has been formalised and 'held' in the 14 'stations' that can be seen around the walls of Roman Catholic churches (and others), depicting various events on the way from Jesus' trial to his death. The prayerful walking around these images, stopping at each one to be reminded of what it means to 'take up your cross', what it meant for God to 'love the world so much',[38] can be a profound way of 'doing' our formation for living baptism as Christ's dying. But these traditional 14 stations are only one possible way of walking this path: it may be that each one of us can identify just a few 'markers' or scenes from Christ's Passion, that we can use to map out a walk, a *via crucis*, for our own physical prayer, as we walk through our neighbouring streets, or on a favourite piece of countryside, or just around our garden. Perhaps there are ways of praying a *via crucis* on our journeys to work!

FORMATION IN PRAYER

Silent, contemplative prayer before the cross or crucifix has its own particular power to form us, without words or even thoughts, into men and women strengthened to live the mystery of Christ's cross. There are times, too, when that deep prayer of silence is hard to arrive at, and we need good words to draw us into it – words which have been forged in the lives of those who have, themselves, lived this daily denying of self; words which make us safe to be fragile enough to be broken open to the power of Christ's death, and let it transform our lives. We might find these looking through books of prayers, or by looking through the various church liturgies for Good Friday, Passiontide, and Easter. We might find blessed words, too, in those sections of hymn books headed 'Christ's suffering and death' or 'Passiontide' and so forth. The following prayer of John Wesley is a powerful example of words which can open up a time for silent meditation on the cross:

> O Jesus, poor and abject, unknown and despised, have mercy on me, and let me not be ashamed to follow thee.
>
> O Jesus, hated, calumniated and persecuted, have mercy on me, and make me content to be as my master.
>
> O Jesus, blasphemed, accused, and wrongfully condemned, have mercy on me, and teach me to endure the contradiction of sinners.
>
> O Jesus, clothed with the habit of reproach and shame, have mercy on me, and let me not seek my own glory.
>
> O Jesus, insulted, mocked, and spit upon, have mercy on me, and let me not faint in the fiery trial.
>
> O Jesus, crowned with thorns and hailed in derision;

O Jesus, burdened with our sins and the curses of the people;
O Jesus, affronted, outraged, buffeted, overwhelmed with injuries, griefs and humiliations;
O Jesus, hanging on the accursed tree, bowing the head, giving up the ghost, have mercy on me, and conform my whole soul to thy holy, humble, suffering Spirit.[39]

DAILY DYING, AND DEATH AS DAILY

Perhaps the greatest challenge in growing more fully into a baptismal living of Christ's death, is that of allowing it to be ever more present to us in the way we speak, the things we do, the choices we make. Prayer, Scripture, and worship in church are essential for this; but so, too, is the regular calling to mind of the way of life that has been set before us in thinking about the cross. Allowing our lives to be regularly questioned by this reality of baptismal faith will bring about small and significant changes. The sorts of questions we might habitually ask are:

- Where do I see the 'martyrdom of love' in my own life – that denial of my own immediate desires, when faced with the need of another? When my children, my partner, my friend – or my enemy! – asks something of me, do I think first of my own convenience, my own plan, or can I give way in love to that person, meeting Christ in that moment?
- In the shape of my day, what place does my own comfort and pleasure and satisfaction have, in relation to the good of others? Do I use 'free time' well?
- When things are hard – I'm not well, or hungry, or tired, or worried about work, or money, or family – at these times, how do I respond to the 'crosses' I'm having to bear? Do they send me back to the Lord? Or do they push me into a place of anger, or complaint to others, or self-pity?
- What place do I find in my affection and care, and in my prayer, for the dying, the suffering, the tortured, and the bereaved? When these things touch my life, how do I respond to them?
- Do I live and plan my life as if this here-and-now existence is everything to me? Or are my choices and plans made in the knowledge that this life, and its rewards and pleasures, are pro-

visional, and that there is nothing compared to love of and in Christ?

This is a hard interrogation; these are hard things to reflect on. But the power of the cross of Christ is at the heart of baptismal living. This, after all, is what it means to be fully human, to love without anxiety, to be completely free in the knowledge of God's promise to us. If we are ever once brave enough to try it, we will know, with the saints, that there is real joy and peace here. Because this is where Jesus, the crucified, is; it is where we are called to be close to him.

CHAPTER SIX

BAPTISM AS THE WOMB: SHARING IN CHRIST'S RESURRECTION

> *Do not be astonished that I said to you, 'You must be born from above.'* John 3:7, Jesus' words to Nicodemus

> *He saved us ... through the water of rebirth and renewal by the Holy Spirit.* Titus 3:5

> *God raised Jesus Christ from the dead*
> *and sent the Holy Spirit to recall the whole world to himself.*
> *In baptism we die to sin and rise to newness of life in Christ.*
> *Here we find rebirth in the Spirit,*
> *and set our minds on his heavenly gifts.*
> *As children of God, we are continually created anew,*
> *as we walk the path of faith ...*
>
> From the Introductory Prayer for Baptism celebrated in Eastertide, *Common Worship*

There has been a certain strain felt in the previous chapter. By focusing on the way in which the baptismal tradition speaks about sharing in Christ's death, we have been constantly, implicitly, brought up against the faith that says that his death was not the end; the previous chapter's theme pressed hard, all the time, against the themes of this chapter. This is hardly surprising. After all, the *only* reason we can know Christ's cross in the way that we do is because of the light shone on it by his resurrection. Not that the resurrection is some kind of 'happy ending' to the Passion; rather it is the living witness to the truth of our being saved by Christ's cross, in a way that is obscured by the sheer horror and hardness of the story of Christ's suffering and death. More than that, even; the resurrection is the breaking through of God's glory, his eternal life, the things of heaven, into our world and history, such that this same human place can never be the same again. Living baptism means living this reality of resurrected life.

For if the tradition is clear that baptism makes us sharers in Christ's death, this is always held together with our sharing in his resurrection. This becomes compellingly clear when we look at the extended quote from Paul's letter to the Romans, with which our last chapter was headed:

> Therefore we have been buried with him by baptism into death, so that, just as Christ was raised from the dead by the glory of the Father, so we too might walk in newness of life. For if we have been united with him in a death like his, we will certainly be united with him in a resurrection like his.[1]

The cross-bearing call of baptismal living is always and intimately bound up with this power of new life in Jesus Christ, who is risen from the dead.

This theology of baptism as a sharing in Christ's resurrection can be seen in a number of images of baptism. So we find baptism understood in the early Church writings and liturgies as a point of new birth, regeneration – the coming to be of a new life. (The much later tradition of Easter eggs can be seen as a rather tasty echo of this!) One of our earliest sources for reflecting on baptism, Justin Martyr (around AD 160), characterises baptism as being 'reborn';[2] and a third-century prayer at baptism names this as 'the laver [washing] of regeneration'.[3] Baptism is about the living of the new life of Easter; hence the medieval tradition of understanding the font as the 'womb' of the Church, the place out of which we are born as God's children. It is for this reason, too, that the Roman Catholic *Rite of Christian Initiation of Adults* argues for the baptism of catechumens to be normally at the great celebration of Easter, the Easter Vigil, in which the new waters are blessed, and the new Easter light is kindled.[4] This practice is, itself, a rediscovery of the ancient practice of Christians, and a testimony to that extraordinary teaching of Jesus to Nicodemus, where we are told that we must be 'born again', born of 'water and the Spirit'.[5] This key text is taken up in the introductory prayer to baptism in *Common Worship*:

> Our Lord Jesus Christ has told us that to enter the kingdom of heaven we must be born again of water and the Spirit, and has given us baptism as the sign and seal of this new birth.[6]

This long and constant tradition which sees baptism as new birth, the start of life in Christ and a participation in his baptism, demands that we deepen our understanding of this mystery so as to better live our baptisms here and now. We should note, too, that this language of regeneration, of new birth, is bound up in the language of the Holy Spirit, from its scriptural roots in John 3, through to the contemporary liturgical rites. To begin to understand life in the risen Christ is to be drawn into reflection on life 'in the Spirit'. The Trinitarian patterning of baptismal life begins to make itself felt again.

EXPLORING THE TRADITION

EASTER: A SHORT STORY OF CONTINUITY AND DISCONTINUITY

The Gospel narratives concerning the Easter story are some of the most vexed and contentious in modern biblical scholarship. As we have already mentioned, it seems likely that Mark's Gospel – generally supposed to be the earliest to be written – did not originally include an account of the resurrection appearances of Jesus. In our own times this strange-seeming omission from an early text has led to speculation as to whether this extraordinary thing, the resurrection of a dead man, *could* have happened. Many of us today have been brought up, even within the Christian tradition, with a 'healthy (or *unhealthy*) scepticism' regarding this story, fuelled by hotly and widely debated books,[7] and by high-profile media discussion such as that provoked by the comments of the newly appointed Bishop of Durham, David Jenkins, in the early 1980s.[8] We don't need, here, to return to those arguments – which are now, in any case, perhaps rather dated. But it is worth noting this attitude of scepticism, which is so much a part of our culture. In particular, the motivation for this highly interpretative reading of the Scripture stories seems, in the main, to be a concern for making the whole business more plausible, more believable. Frankly, we find the resurrection incredible. We just can't get our reasonable, scientifically informed, modern and rational heads round it: so there must be another way of looking at it. Dismissing the old-fashioned story, we can ask, 'What *really* happened?' and come up with something altogether more sensible and reasonable, secure in our knowledge that, of course, God can't just turn things upside down.

We do like things to add up.

Such is the sceptical argument. And, of course, it is possible to believe that Jesus is still alive *in some sense or other* in a way which does not necessitate belief in his bodily resurrection, and which enables, in practice, participation in the Christian community. But the witness of the Christian tradition has been stubborn in its assertion of the resurrection of Jesus from the dead, the empty tomb. This determination to preach such an unbelievable message is odd. After all, the resurrection was just as hard to believe, to rationalise, to make sense of 2000, or 1700, or 500 years ago, as it is now. Dead people do not come alive again, back into time and space; they are not returned to history in this way. Except, our faith tradition tells us, in this one case of Jesus. Once again we find ourselves troubled by mystery.

It is very hard to know quite what to say about the resurrection. I have never, for example, heard a really fine piece of preaching on Easter day. But this is, I think, the nature of the mystery here. Easter is not so much about a teaching, as a *meeting* – an alive, and enlivening meeting with the One who was crucified, who really died. The Easter stories remind us of something important and true about our Christian faith:

> The gospel we preach is not about memories or ideals or profound thoughts. It contains all these things, but what it is about is the human person, Jesus, alive and present to us and loving us from his human heart. Our Easter faith is that we really do encounter Jesus himself: not a message from him, or a doctrine inspired by him, or an ethics of love or a new idea of human destiny, or a picture of him, but Jesus himself.[9]

This meeting changes everything, and sets our story – indeed, history – off in a new direction. But in itself the meeting is odd and disorientating. It is, after all, a complete reorientation of ourselves in relation to the world and to God, in relation to our own living and dying. Encounter with the living Jesus, risen from the dead, is, as we shall see, marked by some confusion – and by the company of angels.

The shorter, probably original, ending of Mark's Gospel (ending at 16:8) ends with a clear witness to the empty tomb and the resurrection. The women are greeted by the mysterious, angelic figure, who declares, 'He has been raised; he is not here.'[10] But this clear message is met with a note of confusion and anxiety from the women themselves, who are silenced by their own terror and uncertainty. This is the final note, it would seem, of Mark's original story; and, although in the other Gospels it is not fear and failure that end the narrative, all the same, the reaction of confusion and a troubling of spirit when meeting with the resurrection event are consistently seen.[11] In Luke the women, telling their amazing tale, full of terror, are not at first believed; and in Matthew's account we hear that these women, the first witnesses to the resurrection, are filled with 'fear and joy'. A traumatic and troubling combination of emotions, I would have thought!

Perhaps most compelling of all is the story in John's Gospel of Mary Magdalene, who remains weeping at the grave. Having seen the empty tomb, she is, understandably, at a loss what to do next. She had, after all, prepared to do that last act of love and friendship, grieving at the burial place; and now there is not even a place to grieve – even his body is taken from her. It is in this place of tears that she unknowingly addresses Jesus as the gardener. It is only when he speaks her name – 'Mary!' – that she recognises him.[12] In the tears, and the naming of friends, Mary meets Jesus, risen from the tomb, and becomes the first of a history of witnesses to cry out, 'I have seen the Lord!'

There is in this story from the Fourth Gospel a certain theme of problematic recognition which appears in other stories surrounding the resurrection. The disciples who meet Jesus on the way to Emmaus have an entire conversation with him over a number of miles, and fail to recognise him. It is only when they sit to eat, asking him to stay, offering the stranger on the road hospitality – only then do they recognise him, 'in the breaking of the bread'.[13] When the risen Christ meets with his friends by the sea of Tiberias, they again fail to recognise him, until the extraordinary gathering of fish echoes with what they had known of Jesus. They recognise him in this disruptive blessing of their attempt to return to normal life; they eat with him, and know he is the Lord.[14]

The risen Christ is just as much a trouble and a worry to the disciples as the condemned and dying Jesus, it seems! Thomas can hardly be labelled 'doubting', when all he quite reasonably demands is that this properly unbelievable, totally outside-the-normal event, is presented to him in terms of real, bodily encounter. No 'spiritualising', no 'mythologising' of the experience of others will do when it comes to Thomas' faith in the resurrection: Thomas knew Jesus as a man, albeit a somewhat remarkable man; this man died, and he grieved over this, hurt and bewildered by it. That he should be alive with a new life, a resurrected life – this, too, had to be a part of Thomas' real, lived experience.[15]

Somehow – and there are ways named and recognised in the Christian tradition – the living of baptism has to know itself as formed and informed by this living, personal (and so 'bodily') encounter with the risen Lord. But we needn't expect this meeting to be straightforward, or obvious, or a moment of clearing up difficulties, or simply doing away with grief. The resurrection is a real demand on us, as for those first witnesses. The encounter with the risen Lord, whilst absolutely necessary, is also fearful, bewildering, disorientating, and sets up new problems of its own. Not the least of these new questions is, what happens next?

EASTERTIDE: THE LONG STORY OF ABSENCE AND PRESENCE

In all the Gospels the stories of the post-resurrection Jesus appear fragmentary, with little of the sense of connected narrative that shapes the rest of the Gospel story. The sheer strangeness of what is met with in the resurrection is something to do with this. Whatever the real continuity between Jesus before the cross, and the risen Jesus – and the stories are clear that there is such continuity, as we have seen – there is also an abiding sense that the relationship that the disciples have with him is quite different from before. For one thing, the risen Jesus does seem to pop up out of nowhere and then go away again! Jesus is still present to his friends, but not quite as he used to be.

We can only speculate – or, better, meditate on – how the disciples understood what was going on through those days of appearances after the resurrection. If, indeed, they *understood* anything much; the whole thing is too wildly beyond human knowing for understanding to be our main concern. But something of their thinking is hinted at in the story of Jesus' ascension, as we find it in Acts.[16]

This is such an odd, and rather sad, story. In it we see Jesus taking a rather abrupt and peculiar leave of his disciples. And the poignancy of the departure is heightened by the apparent anticipation of great things that the disciples had. As they gather, their first question is a 'What next?' question, loaded with a certain kind of expectation: 'Lord, is this the time when you will restore the kingdom to Israel?'[17] Not an unreasonable hope, really. After all, a holy man, a miracle worker, God's anointed (Messiah) had *risen from the dead*! Great things could and must be expected for the coming time, for the next step in history.

Of course what happens is – Jesus leaves them, completely. They are left, rather foolishly, gazing skywards; and only the company of angels – so often around at these bewildering moments of resurrection living! – brings them back down to earth. And the place where the angels direct the gaze of the bereft disciples is not up into the sky, but back home.

There is something about this hanging about after ascension which seems to me a characteristic of post-resurrection discipleship, and so a characteristic of baptismal vocation. Having been pretty astonished by the resurrection, the disciples are ready for anything, looking for the big event. What they get is a second separation, even a second period of loss, as Jesus, returned to them from the grave, leaves them completely. There is not (immediately) the next big thing. What there is, is a waiting together in the upper room, for something half-known as a promise, and less than half understood – the Holy Spirit. And they do the only thing they can do: pray.[18] The living of baptism is marked by such times, too.

What *does* happen next is, in the end, bigger than any of the greatest ambitions and hopes surrounding Jesus: the sending of the Holy Spirit 'in power', as the determining force and energy for the new life of the new people of God. For baptismal living to be the life of resurrection, it must be life lived 'in the Spirit'.

THE ETERNAL EASTER

We have already seen how the baptismal language of regeneration and new birth is tied up not only with the language of resurrection, but with that of the Spirit, also. When Jesus speaks to Nicodemus of being 'born again', it is, significantly, a new birth 'by water and the Spirit'. Emerging from the 'tomb' of the baptismal waters in order to share Christ's glory, is about being called to live life ever more deeply 'in the Spirit'. The coming of the Holy Spirit is intimately connected with resurrection. It is not for nothing that the liturgical tradition of Christianity sees in Pentecost, and its celebration of the Spirit, the culmination, the 'end' of the Easter season:

> Anyone who does not have the Spirit of Christ does not belong to him ... If the Spirit of him who raised Jesus from the dead dwells in you, he who raised Christ from the dead will give life to your mortal bodies also through his Spirit who dwells in you.[19]

Jesus, who left his friends gazing up in bewilderment and loss at the sky, this Jesus who appeared so absent after his ascension, is become newly and more deeply present in the Spirit. For what the presence of the Holy Spirit enables is a new and greater intimacy – an indwelling, and a sharing of life.

Wherever we come across it in Scripture and the later traditions of Christianity, life in the Spirit is characterised by a principle of reconciliation, of holding together. The most obvious sense of this is the way in which, especially in St Paul's writings, we see the gift of the Holy Spirit as drawing all things and people together in Christ: the body of Christians is one in all its variety of gifts and temperaments because 'in the one Spirit we were all baptised into one body ... we were all made to drink of the one Spirit';[20] 'there is one body and one Spirit ... one Lord, one faith, one baptism ...'[21] Because of the unity of the Spirit, which is God's creative power of grace in the world – because of this, all the varied glimpses of the Spirit are seen as united – across all peoples, all differences, and all apparent disunities.

This important and key aspect of our understanding of the Spirit – our 'pneumatology' – can, however, simply become a disposition to affirm everything, and to deny conflict and difficulty. If we only do this, then we will have forgotten that life in the Spirit is participation in Christ's risen life – the life of the One who brought not peace, but a sword,[22] and who ended up suffering the death of a criminal on the cross. The Holy Spirit not only unites us to one another in our baptism, and in our goodness as God's creation; above all, and primarily, the Spirit unites us with Christ's life – his troublesome message and ministry, his death and resurrection. Indeed, as one contemporary theologian writes:

> The most profound connection ... between our Christian baptism and that of Jesus himself is the gift of the Spirit.[23]

The Holy Spirit is not some vague, divine, good spiritual force. The Holy Spirit is part of the name of God, who is revealed in Jesus. It is this Spirit, the power of Jesus' earthly ministry, the power that drives him to the cross, and by which he is raised from the dead – *this* is the troubling gift of Pentecost, and the principle of the baptismal living of the resurrection.

Just how troubling this is can be seen when we consider the way in which the Spirit draws all things together across space *and time*. In a profound way, life in the Spirit makes us participants in Jesus' life and ministry, his saving death on the cross, and his resurrection. The Holy Spirit is the abiding reality of Trinity, living in us. This is the sharing of Christ's risen life. Nor is this a participation in past events, or simply a blessing of our future. More than this, the Spirit draws us on, uniting us to a reality of the future as well as of the present – the eternal life of heaven, 'the communion of saints'. To live our baptism as 'life in the Spirit' is to live in a sharply alive present moment, which knows its truth only through the 'past' events of Jesus' life. But in this way our very present is held essentially open to God's future, the *eschaton*, or end time, when all will be summed up in Christ.

In the Spirit – in the life of resurrection – human history has already been accomplished. It is for this reason that the first Christians understood themselves as 'pilgrims', people with no settled home here on earth, for whom this present life was a sometimes joyful, sometimes hard, journey towards the 'heavenly Jerusalem'. Living life in this 'eschatologically sensitive' way – in a way constantly pulled towards God's ultimate (last) plan for humanity, the *eschaton* – living this baptismal grace means setting our eyes on 'the things of heaven' as our most real basis of life and being. This is what participation in Christ's resurrection means:

> If you have been raised with Christ, seek the things that are above, where Christ is, seated at the right hand of God. Set your minds on things that are above, not on things that are on earth, for you have died, and your life is hidden with Christ in God. When Christ who is your life is revealed, then you also will be revealed with him in glory.[24]

Our true reality, as women and men baptised into the life of the Trinity, is a hidden matter which, none the less, draws us inexorably towards 'glory' – the life of God, with God. We often hear talk, in our own culture, of 'real life' or 'reality TV' – usually referring to the nitty-gritty, the mundane, the ordinary and everyday. Well, the Holy Spirit certainly affirms this as 'real' – it is, after all, created by God, and is *the* place of revelation, of God becoming man in Jesus. But the Spirit, and our call to live in the Spirit, reminds us, too, that all *this* 'reality' is, ultimately, to give way to God's greater reality. Through baptism our 'real life' is hidden with Christ. Such a faith, if fully appropriated, must surely make a difference to our everyday living.

'THE WHOLE PROBLEM WITH THE HOLY SPIRIT'

It would be wrong, I think, to leave these reflections on life in the Spirit without some mention of what I rather recklessly tend to call 'the whole problem with the Holy Spirit'. For there is a danger, in much of what has been said so far, that we can read this living of resurrection as something too personal, too much to do with *me-and-God*. In fact, as some of the earlier references to St Paul's understanding of the Spirit make clear, the Holy Spirit is never 'mine', or any one person's. The Spirit is radically free, blowing where he will.[25] It is because of this free giving of gifts that we experience the Spirit not only as a reconciling and uniting power, but also as the divine principle of a certain diversity and controversy in baptismal living. The Holy Spirit causes trouble, for us sinful humans, at least!

Paul's image of the body in 1 Corinthians 12 speaks eloquently of this. Here the Apostle describes the necessary diversity of gifts and function in the body of Christ – the Christian community. This diversity is *itself* a gift of the one, unifying Spirit who holds all this diversity in unity together, drawing it toward the one God. The Spirit freely gifts Christ's people; which is lovely, I suppose, until I find that he does it in ways that often seem quite inappropriate to me, and to others, and to the leaders and elders of a community! If the Spirit is the living power of the risen Christ among Christians, it is not surprising, given what we're like, that we spend quite a lot of time trying to tame, pin down, or lock up that power. After all, God doesn't see things the way we do; so to allow his real presence to be the governing power of the community is opening a way for all sorts of difficulty and argument.

The Holy Spirit becomes, then, something of a difficulty for Christians, especially as we try to organise ourselves, and have rules and certainties, things that make the mystery add up. One of the earliest experiences of schism, of communities being split, in the Church revolved around this troublesome faith in the freely gifting Spirit. Indeed, this seems to be the problem in Corinth to some extent; but in the second-century schism of Montanism we see an articulate struggle over how the power of the Spirit was to be recognised in the Church. If these women, Priscilla and Maximilla (and I think it is significant that they are women) can go about claiming authority because of a gift of ecstatic prophecy, and gather people about them ... well, how is such an unruly giftedness to be managed?[26] The faith that the Spirit allows the Lord's voice to continue to be heard, and that this Spirit cannot be pinned down – this is a faith which leads us into a life of disturbance, and discernment.

In various ways this question persists down to our own day – in parish arguments, in church questions about who is to be heard and why, and, painfully, in ecumenical disagreements. If it is really true, as we believe, that the Spirit is given to the whole Church, and to each member in it, as the indwelling of the risen Lord, and as the Advocate who will lead us into all truth – well then, how is this truth and this life to be discerned amid all the human opinion, failings and misunderstandings? Different Christian communities have, traditionally, given different responses to this – through appeal to someone 'in authority', by a certain kind of use of Scripture, by seeking consensus of common opinion. None of these alone quite fits the troublesome truth about the Spirit. For the thing is that living in the Spirit means being open to God's real and powerful presence in a world which has seen his sharing of human life and death, and his victory over death in the resurrection. This presence of absolute divine mystery among us can hardly be expected to easily translate itself into clear opinions, rules, teachings, without ambiguity or difficulty!

Faith in the Spirit is demanding. It involves us in discernment, and controversy. Living baptism as life in the Spirit requires both courage to speak, and the humility to listen.

LIVING THE MYSTERY

I've suggested in this chapter that living the risen life of baptism, which can be understood as life in the Spirit, is a call to look beyond the here and now, which we tend to think of as our only or chief reality, and be reminded of our call to eternal life, to contemplate the things of heaven. This is, I am sure, an entirely traditional way of understanding Christian discipleship, rooted in the scriptural testimonies, and in the historical living out of Christianity in the Church. It is characteristic of those acknowledged for their sanctity that they look to God's promise for the future. In a passage on the Holy Spirit, St Paul reflects this when he writes:

> I consider that the sufferings of this present time are not worth comparing with the glory about to be revealed to us.[27]

Christians are a people 'not of this world', even while thoroughly in it. It is this that frees us to love with Christ's love, and live an active hope for all humanity.

But if this is, in fact, 'traditional Christianity', it is also, for us today, somewhat counter-cultural. Many of us are – perhaps rightly – uncomfortable with anything that emphasises the 'next world' rather than the here and now. We are wary of any 'spiritualisation' of human destiny that might lead to a neglect of the poor, the oppressed, the needy in this world. To be truthful, we are also put off by the idea of holding our own needs, comforts, present ambitions in question, in the way that these eschatological, resurrection reflections suggest. Nor are we as comfortable with the troublesome freedom of the Spirit as we are with our own reassuring certainties and opinions. On the whole, we have good reasons to love the world, to hold onto life and its good things, including our own common sense. We find the imagining of something better or truer further on, or further up, just about impossible.

And so it is. If we think that resurrection living is a faith we can *imagine* ourselves into, then we've missed the point. It is a reality born out of the disorientation of encounter with the living Christ as a bodily, here-and-now reality. This is a faith born out of the indwelling of the Holy Spirit, with all the turbulence and consolation, controversy and hope, diversity and unity, that this brings. This is a living which frees us to affirm and celebrate what is good in God's world, and to work in love for the good of others, *precisely because* we have the promise of this all being drawn together in God. Because we know the world's 'end' (or goal, or culmination – *telos* in the Greek) is to be the glory of heaven, we cannot help but love it as the anticipation and place of revelation, of that destiny. But to know this is hard; and it requires a formation of faith in prayer, study, thoughtfulness and daily practice, if it is to become an effective part of our baptismal living.

SHAPING OUR THINKING THROUGH SCRIPTURE

There is a real sense, of which we are vividly reminded by the great Reformation theologian Calvin, in which the Holy Spirit is always to be present to us in the authentic reading of the Scriptures. To pray, before our reading, that the Spirit should guide our understanding and thinking through the Bible passage we have chosen, not only reminds us of this, but also, surely, opens up our minds and hearts more to the power of the Spirit. And, in his Spirit, we can be sure God longs to respond to our invitations. It is with this sense of allowing the Spirit to form our minds in tune with Scripture that the following readings are suggested as ways into deepening our sense of the mysterious, resurrection, eschatological living with which we have been concerned here.

There are, of course, the Gospels' resurrection stories themselves, with all their humanity and consternation, and joy mixed with fear. These are, we need to know, the characteristics that attend a true meeting with the risen Christ. Here is a selection:

- Luke 24:1–12: the women at the tomb.
- John 20:1–18: Mary meets with the risen Christ.
- Luke 24:13–35: the stranger on the road to Emmaus.
- John 20:19–23: the risen Lord communicates the Spirit.

Then there are passages which speak vividly of the living of risen life, as a living in the Spirit, orientated to future glory with God:

- John 3:1–8: Jesus speaks to Nicodemus about being 'born again', by water and the Spirit.
- Romans 8:12–39: a long passage, but worth taking as a whole, slowly, or broken up into sections. A vivid testimony to life in the Spirit, its connection to the life of Christ, and its call to the things of heaven.
- Colossians 2:8—3:4: rooted in a reflection on baptism, this calls us to a discernment of the things of this world in the light of our future life with Christ in God.

SIGNS AND SYMBOLS

I suppose it is hardly surprising if finding signs and symbols to remind us of the resurrection and the Holy Spirit and life everlasting is a bit trickier than finding symbols of Christ's death! There is something *essentially* hidden about resurrection and Spirit: no one witnesses the resurrection as such – only the fact that Jesus, who was crucified, dead and buried, is living. Angels are bumped into, lives are transformed, and meals are eaten with the risen Lord; but this is a mystery hard to embody.

One of the traditional ways in which the Easter mystery and life has been represented in the Christian liturgical tradition has been through the use of candles, specifically the use of candles in darkness. More specifically still, it is the great Paschal or Easter candle, which is central to the Catholic solemn celebration of Easter, that stands as the sign of risen life. So it is that the first action of the celebration of Easter in the Roman Rite is the lighting and blessing of the new fire, which is used to light the Paschal candle. As this candle is solemnly brought into a completely dark church, 'Christ our light' is intoned. And, slowly, falteringly, each person present is given a share in that Easter light, lighting their candles from the

Paschal candle. As the dark church fills with this people of baptismal, resurrection living, it fills with warmth and light.

The telling of this bit of liturgical practice is done to highlight the ways in which lighted candles – especially in dark places – can speak to us of Easter living, of Christ our light. This symbolism can readily be brought into our homes: lighting our evening place of prayer by a single, specially marked-out candle; decorating a candle, or painting a candle dish or holder, with images that speak of resurrection – the empty cross, the burial clothes, the signs of new life of the Easter garden. Light, especially light supplied by fire, is, after all, mysterious. In a culture where we take completely for granted the flicking of a switch for the lighting up of a whole room, the reminder of a primary, mysterious and elemental source of light in the flame can become a powerful symbol to us of our 'real life ... hidden with Christ in God'.

We might also ask ourselves about the images with which we fill our houses, and so our imaginations. Coming from a tradition in which statues and images of saints are the norm, I am aware how much their presence around the place acts as a vivid, deeply human reminder of resurrection, and the eternal life into which the Spirit draws us. Whether in my home, or in church – Our Lady, Joseph, St Therese, St Catherine, St Francis – all these images remind me of 'friends in heaven', and so of the place to which my baptism directs me, too. They are, in their humanity-like-mine, their failings and sins, reminders of that greater community of holy living, beyond what I normally think of as church, or parish, or neighbours. Their having gone before is both an encouragement, and, sometimes, a fearful reminder of God's promise and future, anticipated (albeit often half-heartedly) in my own living of baptism.

I can imagine not all Christians would feel this comfortable with images of the saints in their home or place of work. But perhaps this is an ancient tradition which can be adapted and so more widely adopted: a photograph of Dietrich Bonhoeffer, or John Paul II; a copy of a Renaissance painting of the nativity, or a depiction of the resurrection itself; one of the many copies of Eastern Orthodox icons – these and other images can work as signs that refer our present here-and-now sense of reality to that eternal reality of the fullness of resurrection life. There are, after all, a crowd of witnesses to heavenly life in human history; their presence to us, in pictures, or in getting to know about their lives, can be a window onto that reality of which our baptismal life in the Spirit speaks.

FORMATION IN PRAYER

I have sometimes been asked a rather odd, and not, in the end, terribly useful question, about *who* I pray to: is it to the Father, or to Jesus, or to the Holy Spirit? It is a strange enquiry, and troubles me for the way it seems to suggest that these are distinct *people* to whom we address ourselves, rather than the one God, revealed to us in the name of Father, Son and Spirit. The need to pattern our prayer in keeping with this Trinitarian mystery is witnessed to in the public liturgical prayer of the Church, where the one God is addressed, by praying *to* the Father, *through* the Son, and *in the power of* the Spirit. This is, in fact, the pattern offered to us by Paul:

> When we cry, 'Abba! Father!' it is that very Spirit bearing witness with our spirit that we are children of God ... joint heirs with Christ ...[28]

With, and because of, Jesus we can call God Father; and when we do so we are alive in the Spirit.

For all this there is, too, a tradition in the Church of calling specifically on the Spirit, as the living presence of God among us. This calling of the Spirit into our lives is a prayer to be led out from ourselves into a deeper living of Christ's risen life. It is a 'praying in', a letting in through prayer, of the *telos*, the end to which God draws us in himself. It's something that can take its own proper place in our life of prayer, whether through the still, quiet and meditative repetition of a simple invocation – 'Come, Holy Spirit!' – or by using one of the ancient prayers to the Spirit that have come down to us through liturgies and hymnodies. This calling on, and waiting for, the Spirit, involves the quiet opening of our time – 15 minutes, half an hour, or an hour – to God's living presence. It is a sure way of nurturing that baptismal gift of resurrection living. Bit by bit, day by day, we learn where our real lives lie, as Christ's glory becomes more vivid to us in these times of prayer.

LIVING 'REAL LIFE'

As these mysteries of life in Christ's resurrection, in the power of the Spirit, become more and more *the* reality of our living, that day-to-day living will, itself, be changed. We can't make this happen; nor, really, can we measure or assess its happening. All we can do is attend to the mystery itself, and note the fruit borne in our lives, giving thanks and rejoicing when we catch a glimpse of the Spirit's work in us. But change there certainly will be! To help us see it, we might ask ourselves certain questions about the ordinariness of our lives:

- How is the 'ultimate reality' of my life in God embodied in the routines of my day? Are there real times for prayer, for letting God's Spirit pray in me? Is there time in the week for worship with other Christians, times when other things are rearranged so as to make worship the priority? Do I enable those I live with to find the space and time they need to be just with the Lord? Do we pray together, or talk about the things of God together?
- How far am I really open to the freedom of the Spirit, and able to recognise him in unlikely people and circumstances? Do I tend to have more time, more listening for some kinds of people than others? And on what basis? Am I prepared to have my own assumptions challenged – by my children, my juniors at work, or by those who I think less of?
- Where do I look in my life for joy, for what is life-giving? Are these 'things of heaven', or are they escape routes, providing only temporary pleasures, and an opportunity to opt out of living for a bit?
- Do I have real, practical ways of honouring the life and goodness of the world, as creation destined for glory with God? What care do I take of this divinely orientated earth and its environment? How do I materially aid others, making more vivid and true the loving plan of God for all humanity?
- Can I change my behaviour – recycling, giving to charity, volunteering for care work – to witness more fully to what is 'really real' in God's world?

Resurrection living seems to me to involve a level of letting go on the here and now, which can be difficult, and which I, for one, am generally reluctant to do. Such a letting go can only really be based on a trust – a trust in God's promise that he has even better gifts for us than the ones we cling to. Living baptism as resurrection is, for most of us, a hard thing to learn; but it is also full of joy. For in it we know that Jesus is closer to us than he could ever have been, even if we'd met him during his life on earth. For now we live in the Spirit, and the Lord has made his home not just with us, but *in* us.[29]

CHAPTER SEVEN

SHARING IN CHRIST'S BODY: A COMMUNION OF SAINTS

As many of you as were baptised into Christ have clothed yourselves with Christ ... all of you are one in Christ Jesus. Galatians 3:27–8

We welcome you into the fellowship of faith;
we are children of the same heavenly Father;
we welcome you.

Common Worship, Rite of Baptism

In telling the theological story of baptism in the last few chapters, we have moved from Jesus' life and death, to his resurrection, and the living of life 'in the Spirit'. It is this life in the Spirit which is always the necessary context in which we think about the community of Christians, 'Christ's body'. Thinking about the risen Jesus' abiding gift of the Spirit draws us, without fail, into the question of how this Spirit is met with, celebrated and recognised; and, in various ways, the answer to this is always 'church'. This chapter takes a closer look at this common ordering of Christian life which is Church.

It is perhaps one of the most humanly touching aspects of the Christian celebration of baptism, that it is frequently accompanied, in the rite itself, by some sign of affectionate welcome. So the Roman *Rite of Christian Initiation of Adults* is begun by a 'friendly greeting' of the candidate for baptism;[1] and the infant in these rites is greeted with the embracing words: 'the Christian community welcomes you with great joy.'[2] Here what is being made clear is that this sacrament has introduced the newly baptised person into the Christian community. At the same time, that community, for its part, has received the newly baptised in Christian love. In the Church we are bound together in Christ, all marked by the sign of the cross. Through the waters of baptism a new Christian comes to birth and shares this life with all of us. This is an event not only in the life of the baptised individual, but a significant moment in the life of the community:

> When we attend a baptism we do not go merely to see a spectacle ... We are gathered around the newly baptised as fellow members of the church. We say to him: 'Now you belong to us, and we to you, in quite a new way.'[3]

Baptism is a moment of mutual responsibility, of mutual participation in a common life – the life of the Spirit.

So we see that baptism joins us to Church, to the human community, and, fundamentally, to the body of Christ. We become members of his body.[4] As John Calvin writes:

> Baptism is the initiatory sign by which we are admitted to the fellowship of the Church, that being engrafted into Christ we may be accounted children of God.[5]

For Calvin, baptism is our admission to the Church. Like joining any group, we make promises, and demonstrate some willingness to abide by rules (like the Creed), we are made welcome by those who are already members, and certain privileges and responsibilities are, from then on, recognised. But the second half of Calvin's sentence makes clear what is *different* here: in baptism, we not only join the fellowship of Christians, but we are 'engrafted into Christ' – we become living parts of Christ's living body, which is the Church. This is also clear in a recent expression of baptism from that most human-looking organisation which is the Roman Catholic Church:

> By communicating his Spirit, Christ mystically constitutes as his body, those brothers of his who are called together from every nation. In that body the life of Christ is communicated to those who believe and who, through the sacraments, are united in a hidden and real way to Christ in his passion and glorification. Through baptism we are formed in the likeness of Christ ...[6]

For both Reformed and Catholic Christianity, baptism is understood as making us members of Christ's body. Indeed, this is firmly rooted in Scripture: in baptism we have all become one in Christ,[7] and our baptism is *one* baptism, just as there is one Lord and one Spirit, one body to which all belong.[8] Baptism is a properly ecclesial, communal matter, and no private affair.

It is for these reasons that, across the Christian communities, there has been a consistent recognition of the importance of the communal celebration of baptism. The earliest rites of the Church of England make this clear:

> Baptism should not be ministered but on Sundays and other holy days, when the most number of people may come together. As well for that the congregation there present may testify the receiving of them that are newly baptised into the number of Christ's church, as also because in the baptism of infants, every man present may be put in remembrance of his own profession made to God in his baptism.[9]

In this celebration the newly baptised is welcomed and received. At the same time all present are made mindful of the mystery and call of their own baptisms. This tradition is confirmed in many contemporary documents across the denominations.[10] Baptism is, then, always a communal celebration, a celebration and a transformation of the whole Church, as the body of Christ grows to embrace and share his risen life with new people. Indeed, strictly it is not 'my baptism' or 'your baptism', but only ever 'our baptism' – our particular sharing and participation in the one baptism which makes us members of the same body.

This is a consideration which is especially important as the context for understanding infant baptism. For it makes clear that *none* of us – adults or babes in arms – makes ourselves members of Christ as a sheer act of reason and will. Rather, the loving grace of God in Christ, to which we are open in our own freedom, and to which we are brought through the love of others, makes us participants in this mysterious communion of Christ's risen life. The verbs we use must be in the passive voice with regard to our humanity: we are joined to Christ's body; we are made members of the Church. This is *God's* act in baptism.

A certain tension characteristic of Christian mystery is in all this. These reflections on Scripture and the baptismal rites speak of how being baptised draws us into the life of a human community, which is *also and at the same time* the body of Christ. The Church is known to us as both human organisation and divine mystery, as, classically, 'visible and invisible'. The living of baptism surely draws us into a need to deepen our understanding of this mysterious reality to which we 'have been belonged'.[11]

Living as a member of Christ's body needs thinking about – as the thoughts that follow show.

EXPLORING THE TRADITION

THE CHURCH AS THE BODY OF CHRIST: A PROBLEMATIC TRADITION OF SCRIPTURE

When we speak, as we have been, of the Church as the 'body of Christ', we are drawn straight back to St Paul's use of this image in his first letter to the Corinthians. Here Paul responds to the sectarianism and vying groups in that community of Christians by reminding them that, in the Spirit, they are one body, indeed Christ's body; all their differences, their diversity of gifts and jobs, are necessary for the health of this precious gift of Christ's presence to the world – a presence that they are called, in baptism, to embody.[12] This image resonates, too, with the Johannine language of the vine: as branches of the one vine, Jesus, the men and women of the Christian community bear fruit precisely in so far as their life is 'organically' united in the one living, growing life of Christ.[13]

These are powerful and important images of Church, speaking eloquently of something more than a structure or institutions. Rather, what we see here is a sharing of life – indeed, it is the sharing of *divine and resurrected* life, no less! – a full and living participation in the life of Trinity, through Jesus. But even within Scripture there are difficulties in knowing quite how to 'translate' this theology into church practice. The trouble is that a group of difficult, flawed men and women are being called together to live and embody the mystery of divine life, the common living of baptism.

When we look at it like this, perhaps it is no wonder that 'being Church' is, in practice, so troublesome. Indeed, it seems it has always been so. The community at Corinth, to whom Paul addresses the profound image of the body of Christ, is one fraught with disagreements, rivalries and wrongdoing. The actual living of 'life in the Spirit' has, for these first Christians, become distorted into a chaotic free-for-all, a lack of order and discernment, and so, in the end, a lack of charity and simple kindness. The image of the community as Christ's body seeks to hold together the power and freedom of the Spirit, with a proper sense of ordered living and worship, and respect for those different and possibly weaker than ourselves.[14] The problem of being Church is evident from the beginning.

It is worth looking more closely at this understanding of the Church as Christ's body – for it is not a simple idea. In particular, we may wonder what it is really saying about the relation of the Church to Jesus Christ: in 1 Corinthians the Christian community *is* Christ's body; but in Ephesians and in Colossians Christ is more clearly described as 'the head of the body', which is the Church.[15] This may appear a small difference of emphasis, or clarification perhaps; but it is one which was to mark the various ways in which this language of 'Christ's body' was taken up by subsequent generations. What exactly can we mean in saying that the Church is 'Christ's body'?

This question, in later debate, has become concerned with to what extent the 'bodiliness' of the Church – its organisation and structures, and leadership – can or should be identified with the body of Christ. To make an absolute and uncritical identity of 'the Church' and 'Christ's body' would be to give this particular organisation and group of people the authority to act *as if they were Christ in the here and now*. This is Jurgen Moltmann's criticism of the Roman Catholic Church (not entirely justified, nor entirely without point): that the description of the Roman Church *as* the body of Christ is in danger of leaving no room for Christ's Lordship *over* the Church, as the head of the body. If we are too eager to identify a particular institution with Christ's body present on earth – a sort of continuation of Christ's bodily life – then we all too quickly imagine that the risen life, life in the Spirit, is bounded by this or that organisation's set of rules, or particular gathering, or set of structures.[16]

This observation is especially pertinent to the living of baptism as a participation in Christ's body. For any over-emphasis on the ecclesial organisation as, simply, Christ's body on earth, runs the risk of suggesting to the 'ordinary' baptised person that their participation in Christ's here-and-now living is about being 'involved in church things'. We will quickly forget, from this viewpoint, that the resurrected body of Christ, in which we share in the Spirit, is *mysterious*, and, in some sense, without boundaries and organisational edges as such. This mystery of resurrection life may be (and I believe *is*) embodied in the historical reality of Church; but it is a reality which is, in principle, open to the greater mystery which lies ahead of all our own history, time and space. It is a body always and everywhere ordered to 'the head' – Jesus Christ, risen, and ascended into heaven. A sharing in Christ's body in baptism is about being joined to a particular community, or organisation; but it is an institutional joining which breaks open again and again to the 'mystical body' of the Church – that 'communion of saints', here and now, and ahead of us in glory.

'COMMUNION': NOT QUITE COMMUNITY

The use of the language of 'communion' in this context is significant. 'Communion' – or, in its Greek form, *koinonia* – has become something of a buzzword in theologies of Church.[17] It has been widely used in a variety of ecumenical statements on Church, from the agreed statements of the Anglican–Roman Catholic International Commission in the 1970s and 1980s,[18] to the more recent World Council of Churches statement on the Church, *The Nature & Purpose of the Church* (1998).[19] In these settings, describing the Church as *koinonia* or communion has proved useful in speaking both of the reality of organisational churches, and of the greater reality of communion in Christ through baptism. It is significant that much of this renewal of language and thinking has come from the influence of Orthodox Christianity in the West.[20]

The blessing of *koinonia* or communion is that, in itself, it is non-controversial. It can be heard to speak both of our intimate participation in Christ's life, and of our deep relationship with each other as sharing the one baptism. These are things which the Christian tradition as a whole can hold to, and proclaim. But, once more, problems begin to come to light when we seek to describe how, *in practice*, this communion is to be lived and expressed. As the 'boxed' text of the World Council of Churches document makes clear, a good deal of difference, and actual disagreement, lies just below the surface of the language of communion.[21]

A key disagreement, or, at least, difference in emphasis, concerns what, in fact, constitutes 'communion'. Is communion primarily a matter of fellowship, of human relationship, built on friendship, 'face-to-face' encounter, and shared purpose? Or is there a sense in which this *communion* is 'mystical' – that is to say, is it primarily about our participation in Christ, through which we have communion with others (whether or not, in fact, we have any usual sense of relationship with them)?

How we respond to these questions affects how we think about Church, and how we participate in it. It affects how we are to live baptism. So, if the emphasis is on communion as *community*, our focus will be on building Christian relationships, in our congregations, and with our neighbours. Worship is likely to be in a context of a friendly knowing, or getting to know, others; and our energies are likely to be given over to social and sociable enterprises. If, on the other hand, the emphasis is first on communion with Christ, we may feel free to be less concerned with these things. We can take part 'anonymously' in the Church's worship, and may see our prayer for our fellows as a way of communion, just as much as coffee after church.

Well, of course, even the most solitary of Christians is commanded to love, to show real practical charity, and use their gifts for the building up of the community; and more 'sociable', group-joining Christians are still commanded to pray, in the secret room of their solitude before God.[22] Still, this is an important difference in emphasis; because, in the end, the way we enter into the life of the Church, the life of baptism together, will inform us as to what, in reality, that life is, and where, in the end, it is to be found.

Perhaps the contemporary danger, across the denominations, is an over-emphasis on human community as the primary expression of our communion in Christ. We risk equating friendly, human relationships – which, after all, can just as often (or more often?) be found in the pub or golf club, or at the mother and toddler group – with that communion which flows from participation in Christ. In doing this we burden ourselves with 'building up community' as our own, human task – putting on events, parties, cups of coffee, all focused on people getting to know each other, and 'deepening relationship'. The trouble is that we may not end up with the welcoming and open Christian community we long for, but a temperamentally matched group of more-or-less extroverts, who, without wishing or intending to, alienate the awkward, the shy, or those who need, for a time, to be left alone. Communion *simply* seen as community turns the Church back into itself, to gaze affectionately at the other faces around the altar, rather than to turn upward to God's mystery and outward to the lost and peculiar, the unpleasant and inconvenient – the non-joining masses. The Church can, in this way, become like other kinds of human organisation and social group.[23]

The challenge of *communion* draws us deeper: yes, welcome, human relationship and friendship are key things for the Church's life; but somehow this all needs to be directed to *life in Christ*, which both transcends and gives true meaning to these human blessings.

ORGANISED FOR COMMUNION

This is, perhaps, the place from which to re-evaluate structures in the Church. So much of what is said about the Church these days is actually about structures, forms of governance, and organisation. We are often in danger of forgetting the proper complexity of Church as *both* an organisation in history *and* the mysterious body of Christ. Yet being mindful of this 'both-and' is crucial; we live our baptisms as members of the whole of that complexity.

In fact, organisation and communion are deeply intertwined in the Church. It is this that led the Fathers of the Second Vatican Council to insist that 'communion' was not 'some vague sort of goodwill', but was, in fact, 'hierarchical'.[24] Communion is not so much about friendliness and being sociable, but about a certain bond towards others, within a structure of common life which is ordered to – which is to say, in the service of – communion with Christ. 'Hierarchical communion' draws on an ancient common sense, still clearly embodied in, for example, Christian monastic communities: that in order to be freed to love those to whom we are mysteriously joined in Christ (many of whom we might find quite repellent!), we need to share a common order, a common pattern and organisation of time, words, modes of behaviour. We need what religious houses call a 'Rule of Life'.

Today, when we hear that word 'hierarchical', or the language of 'rule', we tend to think immediately of power structures, authorities and, above all, being told to do and think things we don't want to do or think. Not surprisingly, we don't like the sound of it. But this was not always the understanding of 'hierarchical': in its original use with regard to Church, it simply referred to that ordering, or patterning of things, our participation in which enabled access to holy things, the things of heaven.[25] To be 'hierarchically ordered' is to be orientated so that the holy things (*hieroi*) are the head, or start (*arche*), of all our concerns. To suggest that communion needs to be 'hierarchical' is to say that it needs to be structured in the sort of way which opens it out to what is beyond its own informal patterns of relationships, human whims, and interest groups. For our loving and friendship to be *Christian* loving, loving with *Christ's love*, it needs to be referred constantly to the bigger mystery.

So it is that the various traditions of Church order and authority remind us of something easily forgotten in today's emphasis on relationships and community. Communion needs structures or patterns of life which orientate it to the mystery in which it must be rooted, and towards which it must strive, if it is really to speak of the body of Christ. Baptismal communion is not, fundamentally, about being friends with, praying with, sharing faith experiences with some other baptised people I get on with. Rather, it's about sharing an intimate communion of life and worship with many people who I'll never know – and a good number who I do know, and rather wish I didn't!

If this is to be spoken of as 'community', then it should be recognised as something of an 'unnatural' community. Being baptised brings us into true intimacy with people we don't 'naturally' feel attracted to, or get along with, or have anything much in common with. Living baptism calls us to a radical re-examination of friendship, attraction, and relationship. This kind of 'unnatural' community of baptism is only possible if it finds ways of opening up these odd, troubled relationships to the one life in Christ of which baptism speaks. In various ways this is what many traditions of Church structure – whether hierarchical or congregational – have sought to embody. But there is another place where this mysterious communion is not only expressed, but made – that holy communion which is the Eucharist.

COMMUNION, EUCHARIST, AND MISSION

Long before Christians had the writings of the New Testament, before clear structures or a canon of Scripture had emerged, they celebrated Eucharist. This 'breaking of bread', in obedience to Jesus' command at the Last Supper, is what held and formed those first Christians as 'the body of Christ'.[26] The Eucharist holds and makes us present to the entire mystery of Christ's humanity, death, resurrection and abiding presence – the very mysteries of baptism! It is properly understood as the birthplace and fount of renewal for the Church.

It is significant that the Christian tradition gives the same name to *both* the Christian community *and* the sacrament of Eucharist – the body of Christ. To celebrate and fulfil the baptismal mysteries in the mystery of the Eucharist is to participate in a particular way in Christ's body. We receive into our own bodies the sacramental body, and so know ourselves joined to Christ's life, in deep and true intimacy. Because we all share in this sacrament, and in this life of Christ, we are, equally intimately, joined to one another as Christ's body, which is the Church. So St Augustine, preaching to Christians in Africa in the early fifth century, can proclaim:

> If you are the body and members of Christ, then it is your sacrament [the sacrament of yourselves] that is placed on the table of the Lord; it is your sacrament that you receive. To that which you are you respond 'Amen' ('yes, it is true!') and by responding to it you assent to it. For you hear the words, 'the Body of Christ' and respond 'Amen'. Be then a member of the Body of Christ that your Amen may be true.[27]

It is this sharing together – with all sorts of people, and in all sorts of moods – in the body of Christ at the Eucharist, which nurtures and makes possible the baptismal vocation to *be* the body of Christ. More than that: in ways which the theological tradition has nobly (though not always very successfully) struggled to articulate, in the Eucharist we have our *bodily* encounter with the risen Christ, which we know as central to the living of baptism. And when we meet with him in this way, despite all the inevitable confusion, uncertainty, and disorientation, we know ourselves as one in him.

In this way the one body of the Church, constituted in the one baptism, is fully expressed and made alive in the celebration of Eucharist. After all, the institution of the Eucharist at the Last Supper, on the night the Lord was betrayed, the night before he suffered, places us at the centre of Christ's saving Passion and death. The Christian tradition which speaks of the 'sacrifice' of Eucharist is a vivid testimony to this: Christ's giving of his own body, and pouring out of blood, is intimately linked with his imminent and saving death on the cross. As a baptised people we have died with Christ in the waters of baptism: this truth of our being is made real ever more fully in the Eucharist.

But if Eucharist makes us ever-present to Christ's Passion and death, it also, unambiguously, proclaims the resurrection, and new life in the Spirit. It is possible for us to be made present to Christ's saving work in the Eucharist precisely because he is risen. Those 'historical events' of his suffering and death are – mysteriously – eternal events, events in God's life. This is the life which we are called to share in baptism, and in which we share together, in a particular and unique way, in the Eucharist. A full living of baptism, living Christ's body, is, in the end, the living of Eucharist.

This doesn't simply mean that living baptism is about going to celebrate the Eucharist frequently; like baptism, Eucharist is not simply a liturgical event, but a call to and empowerment for holy living in our ordinariness. So, in the Catholic Christian tradition it is worth noting that Eucharist is often called 'Mass'. This is a term taken from the very end of the Latin celebration of Eucharist – *ite, missa est!* – the words which dismiss the baptised people, and send them on their way. In this tradition the Eucharist, that holy communion which makes and expresses the communion which is Church, is named by its end-point, its boundary, the point of departure 'into the world'. The Eucharist decentres its own liturgical action: when we 'go to Mass', we go to the place of dismissal.

I mention this as it highlights an aspect of Church, communion and Eucharist which is too often lost sight of: communion – being a part of the body of Christ through baptism and Eucharist – is a *missionary* way of living. The Church, precisely as Christ's body, the communion of divine life, is necessarily turned out from itself, to serve the life of the whole world as Christ to that world. The Vatican's *Congregation for the Doctrine of the Faith* puts it like this:

> Ecclesial communion is at the same time both invisible and visible. As an invisible reality, it is the communion of each human being with the Father through Christ in the Holy Spirit, and with the others who are fellow sharers in the divine nature, in the passion of Christ, in the same faith, in the same spirit ... By means of these divine gifts, which are very visible realities, Christ carries out in different ways in history his prophetical, priestly and kingly function for the salvation of mankind. This link between the invisible and visible elements of ecclesial communion constitutes the Church as the sacrament of salvation.
>
> From this sacramentality it follows that the Church is not a reality closed in on herself; rather, she is permanently open to missionary and ecumenical endeavour, for she is sent to the world to announce and witness, to make present and spread the mystery of communion which is essential to her: to gather together all people and all things into Christ; so as to be for all an 'inseparable sacrament of unity'.[28]

Here the strange nature of Church as mystical body and human organisation is held together, with a profound notion of communion which compels us to live the life of Church (the life of baptism) as 'the sacrament of salvation' for the world. It is in the nature of Church as Christ's body to be of service in this way to the deep needs of all men and women. Living baptism – living Eucharist and Church – is essentially missionary, a calling to serve the salvation of all.

LIVING THE MYSTERY

The ways in which these mysteries of Church are lived out in our lives will depend on all sorts of human, practical and temperamental things. Being more or less introvert or extrovert might determine how we see ourselves participating in Church, and in mission; the day-to-day pressures on our time and energies, with work and family and friendships, will also shape the ways in which we live baptism as members of Christ's body, called to his service of humanity. Real living of mystery can never be reduced to a 'one size fits all' programme of how to do these things.

The danger is, though, either that we will use this practical complexity as an excuse to define living as Church in terms of our own inclinations; or that the sheer burden of this demand and call will leave us unable to see how we *can* respond to this at all, and we will become quiet and complacent about the missionary call of baptism and its need to be fed in the life of the Church. So, for the extrovert, joining sort of person, being Church might be seen, simplistically, as attending two or three church meetings a week, or organising social events for the church community; and for the busy, stressed working parent, being Church, and all that might entail, can be something put off until a quieter time, when the family's grown, or in retirement. Neither of these responses, and none like them, will do, if we are to live baptism as a call to be the Church of Christ. Like baptism itself, being a member of Christ's body is not another activity to be fitted in, but a whole, radically renewed way of human being.

The challenge to each of us reflecting on this aspect of our baptism is: how can this reality of communion be embodied, lived out in every bit of my life? To be sure, some gathering with other Christians, especially around the eucharistic table, seems to present itself as a non-negotiable component. But then what? How are we to learn to be, in Nicholas Lash's words, 'church between Masses'?[29]

What follows are simply some practical suggestions about how we might begin to discern some answers to these questions in our own lives.

SHAPING OUR THINKING THROUGH SCRIPTURE

Before suggesting some key passages that might be a part of such scriptural discernment about living Church, it might be useful to be reminded that Scripture is, itself, a work of Church. The New Testament arose out of the life of the first Christians, who – as they met to celebrate the Lord's Supper, week by week – sought to learn from the 'memoirs of the Apostles'.[30] This growing need to learn from those closest to Jesus' life, ministry, and saving death and resurrection, bore fruit in the writing down, collection, and treasuring of these 'memoirs' – these teachings and stories. Scripture is, itself, a witness to the formation of Church, and a living fruit of the struggle to live communion in Christ.

To recognise this is to be reminded that, when we sit to read and pray the Scriptures, it can never be a matter of simply 'me and God's Word'. These words of the Bible, through which we may faithfully and truly meet God's saving Word, are, none the less, the words of fellow Christians, articulating for us, across the ages, the authentic (and so authoritative) Gospel, of what it is to live as Christians together.[31] These words of Scripture flow from the faithful living of Church, and call us back to such living of baptismal grace.

There are some particular ways in which this profound link between Scripture and the life of the Church can be seen more clearly. The universal Christian practice of proclaiming and hearing passages from the Bible when we gather to worship, makes clear that this is a Word to be heard together; in the middle of our muddled-up, 'ordinary', fractious coming together, we know that God speaks to us – personally, but also, and always, as his one Church, his People.

Small Bible study, faith sharing or base ecclesial groups often gather around Scripture. Here we can be broken open to one another and to the Spirit through God's Word, and hear that revelation in new and enlivened ways through the multi-voiced experience of the Church in conversation with revelation.

The study and prayerful reading of Scripture with a commentary, or readings from wise and holy Christians of the past, join our reflections on Scripture to the wider 'communion of saints'. So, too, does the personal, home-based reading of Scripture which is set for the wider Church's daily prayer and worship, in the Church lectionary or public prayer cycle.

In all these ways, and others, we can be reminded of the ways in which the Word of God is to make progress in our lives, and in our community:

> The Tradition which comes from the apostles makes progress in the Church, with the help of the Holy Spirit. There is a growth in insight into the realities and words that are being passed on. This comes about in various ways. It comes through the contemplation and study of believers who ponder these

> things in their hearts (Luke 2:19, 51). It comes from the intimate sense of spiritual realities which they experience. And it comes from the preaching of those who have received, along with their right of succession in the episcopate, the sure charism of truth.[32]

In conversation with one another, in communion with Christian tradition, we learn and relearn the witness of Scripture, and are enabled to become part of its living, present witness.

So, it seems good to ask ourselves: In what ways do I encounter Scripture communally, as a member of Christ's body, the Church?

Then, of course, within Scripture there are many texts which reflect the themes of this chapter, and which can deepen our understanding of Church, Eucharist, and mission. Here are a few suggestions:

- Matthew 10: a long chapter, drawing us into reflection on what it means to be sent out on Jesus' mission.
- Mark 10:35–45: the nature of ordered relationship among disciples.
- John 15:1–17: the true vine: abiding in Jesus, and finding our unity there.
- Luke 24:13–35: on the way to Emmaus, the risen Jesus is known through conversation about the Scriptures, and the breaking of bread.

And from the epistles:

- 1 Corinthians 12—13: a long passage, but one that speaks profoundly about both the ordering of community, and the fundamental reality of love.
- Colossians 3:1–17: new life, born of Christ's death and resurrection, lived through daily witness and rule.
- 1 Peter 2:1–9: 'living stones', through being close to Christ; both 'life' and 'structure/building'.
- Galatians 3:27–9: all heirs in baptism, with Christ.

The reading, slowly and in still prayer, of these texts can draw us, little by little, into that deeper and more vigorous living of Church which is true to the great mystery of our baptism.

SIGNS AND SYMBOLS

When we think of Church there is one very obvious, concrete symbol – though not one, however, that can be easily brought into our homes! That is, the church building itself – our place of worship. A first question to ourselves here might be – am I there often enough? Can my baptismal vocation be nurtured and strengthened by more regular or frequent gathering together for worship – especially Eucharist – with others? The physical act of getting ourselves to this place, or of popping in when we pass, can be a practical, present part of the fabric of our living, reminding us concretely of our call to be Church. Such visits can change the geography of our daily routine.

The church building itself has things to tell us about being Church and living Christ's mission. The altar, the furnishings, the statues or images – all of these act as powerful witnesses to our common baptism, and the mysteries into which it draws us. In all this imagery there is, too, the simple concrete fact of the seats or pews arranged around the altar and pulpit: the church is a place waiting to be populated, a place which God holds open to be peopled. Even as we sit in such a place alone, we know the church as pregnant with possibility for men and women – each of whom, despite all our quirkiness, faults and unattractiveness, God loves *completely*. And where, as in my own church, candles burn, lit by others who have prayed before me, we can know even the empty church as the place where people bring the desires and needs and thanks of their lives in prayer.

There is, of course, something of a presumption here that a church building might be open to enter, pray in and light candles in. If this is not the case, we may want to ask, as a congregation together, what exactly our closing of this space in between worship is symbolising?

There are also important ways of connecting our 'out of church' lives with that mystery of being Christ's body. The diary of church events from the parish newsletter can find its way into our prayers, by being pinned up in our homes; and speaking to our friends and colleagues about what we heard or did at church on Sunday extends the life of the Christian community in a simple, ordinary (and often effective) way.

Some of our Christian communities have well-defined shapes to their 'liturgical year' – saints' days; or 'seasons' such as Advent in the run-up to Christmas, and Lent, in the six weeks before Easter. The great feasts of the Church and these seasons and days of celebration and remembering can shape our lives and homes beyond the place and time of worship together. So, for example, when Roman Catholics keep Fridays as a day of abstinence together, or when we allow the 40 days of Lenten penance, or the 50 days of Eastertide to really permeate our lives – here there can be a real communion in Christ through shared custom, discipline and celebration, which goes beyond our getting together at one time, in one place. Whatever the particular traditions of our Christian denomination, we might explore how far these really soak through the busy-ness of our lives, making Church a reality beyond meetings and services.

FORMATION IN PRAYER

There is a sense in which there can never be any such thing as 'private prayer'. This is not to say that we should not sometimes – indeed, often – find ourselves alone with God in prayer; the whole of this book presumes such a practice, and calls for it to be continually deepened and expanded into our living. None the less, the mystery of our communion in Christ through baptism also tells us that we are members of one body, and that what affects one 'member' affects the whole.[33]

Perhaps one of the ways this is clearest in Christian prayer is through *intercession*; the praying *for* another is, in a profound, often invisible way, a building up of Church. As baptised people together, we bear one another's burdens in our praying for each other, and letting ourselves be prayed for. There is, too, Scripture tells us, a real power of healing in obeying the Gospel command to 'pray for those who persecute you.'[34]

Being Church between Sunday gatherings might have, as one of its consequences, a regular pattern of daily prayer which includes a space to remember those who need or who have asked for our prayers. In a particular way, our baptismal sense of Church can call us to intercede for our church leaders, our pastors, preachers and teachers. It would seem important, too, in the light of the Gospel, to be especially mindful in our prayers of our 'enemies'; those people, especially in our Christian community, who have hurt us, or who irritate or seem to undermine us, or who we feel are getting things wrong – these people, who share the intimate life of Christ's body with us through our common baptism, are a special place of prayer for us. In this way our prayer, too, becomes peopled with all those whom the love of God desires to draw to himself.

In the end, praying as Church is populated by the whole of creation.

LIVING 'DOMESTIC CHURCH'

Much of what has been said here resonates with the idea of 'domestic church'. This is a term, rooted in patristic writings, which came to the fore in the Roman Catholic Church in the years after Vatican II, particularly in the teaching of Pope John Paul II.[35] This teaching has renewed the sense that we need to find the 'centre' of what it is to be Church not in the structures of governance, or decision-making, not the organisational centre of things, but rather in that place which often looks like the edges of Church: our homes, our households, our family groups.

To live baptism as a call to Church and its mission means, above all, to take up into the heart of our domestic living the truth that *here* there is a true and real sense of being Church. Here it is, after all, that the Church's call to be the 'sacrament of salvation for the world' is most keenly focused, at the place where the churchiness of Church is almost entirely soaked through with the ordinary, the humanly common things of family, relationship, and household running. In our household prayers, our ordering of life, our practice of hospitality, our homes can become 'domestic churches' where we, and our guests, can truly encounter Trinity, and the mystery of salvation.

It should be clear by now, through all that we have explored about baptismal living, that such a transformation of 'ordinary home' to 'domestic church' doesn't just happen. Going to church on Sunday, being baptised, and being hospitable – all good and important things – do not, of themselves, make a visit to our homes an encounter with saving grace! No; there is, rather, a *call* to domestic church here, to which we need to respond by breaking open our day-to-day domestic living to the truth, mystery and worship of the wider Church, the Church of Christ. Only then, in our prayer, and living signs and symbols, and conversation about faith, will we truly be able to recentre the Church on the boundary land of domestic lay living.

This is, after all, what living baptism has called us to do all along.

CHAPTER EIGHT

'WASHED CLEAN'? LIVING AS SAVED SINNERS

> *... you will give knowledge of salvation to God's people, by the forgiveness of their sins.*
>
> Zechariah's prophecy over John the Baptist, Luke 1:77

> *If we say we have not sinned, we make him a liar, and his word is not in us ... But if anyone does sin, we have an advocate with the Father, Jesus Christ the righteous; and he is the atoning sacrifice for our sins ...* 1 John 1:10; 2:1–2

> *... those baptised are pardoned, cleansed and sanctified by Christ.*
>
> WCC Faith & Order Paper 111, Baptism 4

In reflecting on the theology of baptism, we have told the story of God's coming to us in Jesus, his saving death on the cross, and his resurrection, his sending of the Holy Spirit to draw us close to him in the divine life, and his gathering together of a 'royal priesthood, a holy nation',[1] who embody and draw their life from these mysteries. The theological motifs of baptism, as described in the Christian liturgical and doctrinal traditions, tell the story of redemption; this is an account of what it is to be 'saved' by Christ. But in stating this, we come up against some hard questions: from what do we need to be saved? And what difference can 'being saved' make to our lives? These are the questions for this last main chapter.

The point we have now reached calls us to think more particularly about the nature of 'living baptism', as life lived, here and now, in the power of the resurrection. This living is, necessarily, fraught with that *eschatological tension* of life in the Spirit. This is, put more simply, that tension of living the life of heaven, the truth of God's love, in a world gone wrong. And this last point is *the* point here: the world we live in, blessed and beautiful and graced as it is, is also, and at the same time, 'a world gone wrong'. For we can be sure, all in the world is not as God would have it; all in my heart and living is not as God would have it. Living baptism is about living salvation, yes; but it is also, crucially, about living as 'saved sinners'. For in the Christian tradition it is that terrible destructive reality of sin, which leads in the end to death, from which we have to be saved in Christ.

It may, I suspect, seem strange to many Christian readers that we have managed to get so far along in a book about baptism without yet talking much about sin. In many traditions this is the dominant theme when thinking about baptism, with the waters interpreted as a washing from sin (rather than a burial in Christ's death, or the waters of new birth), and the white baptismal garment as a sign of moral purity (rather than the new creation). I was certainly aware, when working pastorally, that a good proportion of non-churchgoers who brought their babies for baptism were still informed, in some vague, un-thought-through way, by the idea that baptism got you into heaven, by 'getting rid of original sin'. Indeed, the rites themselves make clear that baptism involves a rejection of sin, often including formulae for expressing that turning away from evil.[2]

The connection between sin and baptism goes straight back to the baptism of John, who came 'proclaiming a baptism of repentance for the forgiveness of sins'.[3] This call to recognise sin and repent is, in fact, 'the beginning of the good news'.[4] This fundamental idea has persisted through the Christian Scriptures, and is now a mainstream understanding of baptism across denominations, with differing emphases. Indeed, the 'high' baptismal theology of the Roman Catholic tradition sums up this position unambiguously:

> By Baptism all sins are forgiven, original sin and all personal sins, as well as punishment for sins. In those who have been reborn nothing remains that would impede their entry into the Kingdom of God ...[5]

This statement proclaims boldly that the power of baptism is God's act, God's reaching out in love and mercy to humanity's broken state. As such it is absolute. To be sure, he never calls to us other than in our freedom; but even in our persistent disobedience and hardness of heart, his love has the power to overcome sin whenever, in freedom, we return to him. Baptism opens up our living to this real power of love in a unique, essential way, which radically claims to overcome sin.

But what we all know is that, after the celebration of baptism, we go on doing wrong, hurting others, being selfish. My babies were not transformed into angelic, perfect creatures once I'd got them baptised; no more was I then, or now, after more than 40 years of living with baptism. More obvious still, of course, are the huge, glaring faults of my fellow baptised Christians! In view of all this human horror and nastiness, what can it mean to proclaim, with the Christian tradition, that baptism washes us clean from sin? Can 'living baptism' really, in any effective sense, mean living life free from sin?

This is such a crucial matter for us to think through. For if we don't, then we risk everything else that has been said about 'living baptism' becoming merely a matter of personal piety, in the worse sense of holy-sounding, devotional ideas, which lack the everyday wisdom and robustness to be really transformative of living. When we return from our reading, our prayer, from our celebration of Eucharist or church worship, when we go about our 'ordinary' lives, we will meet – again and again – with our own weakness, irritability, unkindness, selfishness, coldness, laziness, and greed. It is this ordinary truth about our human living and relationships which needs to be integrated with the lofty-sounding truths of our faith in Christ. (And there is surely nothing as ordinary as our sin!)

What happens, all too often, is that we find it easier to live in different compartments: there is the churchgoing, devotional, pious me; and the crabby, demanding, opinionated parent, colleague and friend. The failure to bring these things together enables all kinds of self-deceit about the wonderful, and tragic, truth of who I really am: a creature, fallen and broken, who is totally loved by God, for all that. When we compartmentalise our living in this way – the holy me, and the day-to-day me – then our faith simply becomes a hobby: it is the thing we choose to do in our free or leisure time, because, in various ways, it makes us feel better.

Living baptism is, in large part, about growing in the wisdom needed to embody the reality of salvation in a world full of troubles.

Not least among those troubles are our own shortcomings and unkindness. It is about learning to be a 'saved sinner', learning to live in ways that disclose the central mystery of Christian faith – that God loves us.

EXPLORING THE TRADITION

BEING HUMAN AND 'THE PROBLEM OF SIN'

One of the ways in which sin is a problem became clear to me when giving some teaching on the Mass. I was setting out something of the structure of the Eucharist, which usually includes, in the Roman Rite, a 'penitential rite' as one of the introductory parts of the liturgy. In this rite of penance everyone is called upon to examine their consciences, repent of their sins, and ask for God's mercy and forgiveness. One or two of the students were uncomfortable with this. 'The thing is,' one of them remarked, 'all this talk about sin makes me feel like I'm not *worthy* or something.' I was (briefly) speechless: here we were, talking about worship of the living God, the drawing close to the mysterious beginning and end of everything, and there was an expectation that we were quite up to this, and shouldn't be made at all uncomfortable by it. In the end all I could mumble was something along the lines that I was OK with this liturgical pattern because, in fact, I know I'm *not* worthy. But it made me think.

It reminded me of the number of times I have mentioned 'sin' – in teaching, parish talks, even academic papers – and met with disapproval. I have been asked to speak, instead, of 'weaknesses', 'wounds', temperamental differences, quirks and peccadilloes – anything that gets us away from the dark psychological damage of guilt-complexes, low self-esteem, and self-hatred. To speak of sin is, many think, to risk instilling these negative and destructive feelings in people. In our post-Freudian, psychologically aware culture, we are highly sensitive to these dangers, and so we are averse to the language of personal sin, even within church settings. It's notable that the Second Vatican Council, speaking of the human condition to the society of the mid-twentieth century, found it better to emphasise man's inherent goodness, and the tragedy of the 'wound' of the fall, rather than to say too much about sin.[6]

There is good reason for this, of course. But – as I hope will become clear in what follows – the idea of sin which leads to crippling guilt, and a destructive sense of self, is a terrible distortion of the place of sin in the Christian tradition taken as a whole. It is a distortion for which many Christians must be held responsible; great damage has been done because of this bad teaching. But the solution lies not so much in the refusal to speak of sin, as in a clearer understanding of its place in the joyful and hope-filled story of redemption in Christ.

For, like it or not, the language of personal sin and repentance is the very starting place of the Gospel message, and remains at its heart throughout. John the Baptist, the forerunner of Jesus who prepares a way before him, comes proclaiming 'a baptism of repentance for the forgiveness of sins';[7] his whole prophetic mission is the declaration of redemption, 'through the forgiveness of sins'.[8] Jesus' own, original message is summed up in the earliest testimonies as 'repent, and believe',[9] a call to turn away from the wrongs of the past, seek forgiveness from God, and start on a new life. In the Christian Creed we profess belief in the forgiveness of sins; and in that central Christian prayer – the Lord's Prayer – we routinely pray to have our sins forgiven, and are called to forgive the sins of others. Clearly there is something essential to Christian understanding here.

The concern for human bondage to sin is a central theme of Jesus' work. It is not enough that he heals the sick; he also declares their sins 'forgiven', 'let go' (in the Greek *aphiemi*).[10] And, to the horror of the good, pious people, Jesus spends his time eating and drinking with those known to be 'sinners'.[11] In fact, Jesus himself describes his work as focused on, drawn towards, the sinner, the outcast.[12] Sin is an important matter in Jesus' ministry; it is a real thing, from which we need to turn (repent), and from which we need to be freed or let go. Indeed, Jesus relates it to his own death: 'He took the cup ... he gave it to them, saying: "Drink from it, all of you; for this is my blood of the covenant, which is poured out for many for the forgiveness of sins."'[13] The bondage of sin is so real that it takes the suffering and dying of Jesus to make freedom possible. To speak of Jesus' life, teaching and death, means to be able to speak of and know about sin.

Of course, on one level we do all know about sin. At least, we know that things are not right in the world, and that, as far as we can tell, human history has been marked from the beginning by cruelty, greed, oppression, violence and selfish ambition, just as much as it has been made radiant with care, charity, beauty, and liberation. We know, too, that we struggle, often, with our own weaknesses and faults, and with those of the people we share our lives with. There is something wrong here.

It is this sense of 'something wrong' with which the creation narratives of the Jewish and Christian traditions struggle in the book of Genesis. God creates a wholly good world (for everything from God is good), but things are put on the wrong track by the misuse of human freedom, in defiance of God's will.[14] Our freedom, our ability to make choices, to exercise our will, to contemplate things and act upon that thinking – this is the nature of this humanity created 'in God's image'.[15] It is the turning of that freedom away from God, and the making of ourselves as fashioners of the world, that puts things out of kilter, the story tells us.

So it is that human decision and control come to dominate the world, rather than God's; indeed, this is so much the case that large portions of humanity, for large chunks of time, seem able, throughout history, to behave as if there were no God. What the story of our redemption tells us is that God goes on reaching out to his creation: in his prophets, in blessings, in holy men and women – and, supremely, Christians believe, in Jesus. Human beings have brought the terrible presence of sin into the world, through their being untrue to who they are before God. But however terrible this is, the love and goodness of God is greater and more terrible.

We live, then, in something of a mixed world – what Augustine and later theology would refer to as the *confusio hominum*, the confusion of humanity. This is how things are. This is, in part, what Augustine is referring to in his understanding of 'original sin' – the reality of a distortion of God's good creation through the turning aside of human freedom from God, which lies at the origin, at the start of human history, and at the origin of every personal history. This is not something for which we are individually culpable;[16] it is, rather, a true description of that fundamental basis of human living, within which we all find ourselves. At every turn human freedom is confronted with life and death, God's way and our own will and control, grace and sin. But these are decisions that we are often not up to taking, and in our confusion we add to the invidious muddle of the world around us.

Baptism into the mysteries of redemption through Christ claims to free us from death for life, from sin for holiness; but the world in which this happens is, still, a 'fallen' world. And we are a part of that fallenness.

We can, perhaps, take some consolation from the realisation that this apparent mismatch of the claim of baptism and the daily experience of the baptised has always been a trouble to the Church. The growing awareness that, as a matter of fact, human beings were quite capable of some pretty serious wrongdoing even after baptism perplexed the early Church, and led, in the end, to the development of penitential rites – processes through which the sinner could repent, receive forgiveness, and be reconciled to the Church community.[17] The contemporary practice of sacramental or ritual confession in Catholic traditions of Christianity can be traced back to these practices. The Church has always, and still continues to be, concerned over the tragedy (it is nothing less) of the baptised person who turns, in freedom, away from the call to be Christ's body, to live his or her own life in contradiction to the Gospel.

The hard question is how to respond to the tragedy of sin here. There have always been those in the Church who sought to take a strict, perfectionist or rigorist line on this, such as the Montanists in the early centuries, and the Anabaptists during the Reformation. Here right living, moral rectitude, and strict discipline in relation to devotional observances are absolutely necessary to inclusion in the community; the sinner is expelled, for a time, or even altogether. Such a practice suggests that the sacramental bond of baptism can be distorted out of recognition, and even broken, through a person's sin. What we should note, however, is the stronger tradition within Christianity which has always tempered such rigorism with an awareness of our *common* tendency to sin, and, indeed, our common *experience* that we do, in fact, sin. So Augustine, appealing to the Lord's parable of the wheat and the tares, speaks of the Church itself as a *corpus permixtum*, a mixed (even mixed-up?) body,[18] where 'many who appear to be in are out, and many who appear outside are inside.'[19] The true mystery of the body is visible only from the Church's end in God, its fulfilment in Christ at the *eschaton*.

Sin *and* grace are present to us in our living of baptism, in Church and world. Sin *and* holiness are constant and real possibilities for each moment of our own lives. So in what sense can we say baptism 'frees us' from sin?

SIN IN THE LIGHT OF GOD'S GRACE AND LOVE

To go further in understanding this, we need to return to the Gospel, and to the mysteries of our redemption in Christ's death and resurrection. In fact all we really need to do is draw out what has already been said. For it proved impossible to speak of sin in the Gospel without speaking of forgiveness; and impossible to speak of Christ's cross, without the language of God's love and desire to save us. It is impossible, too, to speak of resurrection without knowing this as a victory of God's love and compassion over our death-dealing stubbornness and self-centredness.

In fact sin is central to the Gospel message and story in that it is precisely the place of God's compassion and saving love. The point about 'sinners' being among Jesus' favourites is that they know their need of God, whilst the good and the upright (the Pharisees – like many a 'good Christian') too easily fool themselves into thinking that they are, of their will, 'good'. Why would they need God when they can be holy all on their own? Jesus' biting parable of the Pharisee and the tax-collector praying in the temple vividly illustrates the point.[20] The Pharisee, for all the certainty of his devotional behaviour, and upright life, cannot know God's blessing, for he cannot honestly come before God and make the prayer of the tax-collector: 'God, be merciful to me, a sinner!' When we look back at our reference to the centrality of sin to Jesus' mission it becomes clear that the message is not 'You're all bad people, hopeless sinners', but rather, 'Repent, turn around, and see that God wants to forgive you, to free you in and for his love.' We are not likely to repent and turn to God if we really believe we're pretty much OK on our own.

The personal knowledge of the tragedy of sin, in which all human beings are thoroughly implicated, is, in the Christian Gospel and tradition, the moment when we can begin really to know God's love. Confronted by my own, real and damaging sin, I can fully turn to God, and let him free me from sin's enslavement.

The woman known as a sinner pours out her hopelessness wordlessly, consumed by tears, and only then can she hear not just that she is forgiven, but that she is to be remembered as one who 'loved much': 'the one to whom little is forgiven, loves little.'[21] Here the knowledge of sin, repentance, and forgiveness are set before us as the proper context for Christian love. It is from this difficult place of pain and wrong that we can learn to love much.

This is bad news indeed, for any of us who don't feel the need to be forgiven our sins; for how, otherwise, can we keep the command to love? And how can we know just how loved we are?

It is in this spirit that Christians down the ages have associated the sorrowful 'confession' or acknowledgement of their own personal sins, with the moment of grace when they are freed in truth to praise God, in the great knowledge of his love for us. St Augustine, in his great and extraordinary work *The Confessions* (AD 397–8),[22] intertwines in a compelling and authentic way his praise of God's forgiving love, with the narrative of his life, described in terms of his own sinfulness, coming to conversion, and continuing struggles. For Augustine the knowledge of one's own sin is a necessary part of the truth-telling which is needed in the search for God. For St Catherine of Siena, about a thousand years later, the theme is still fresh; it is in the true knowledge of ourselves as limited, failing, small and sinning, that we can be free to know the love of God. So God speaks to Catherine:

> Here is the way, if you would come to perfect knowledge and enjoyment of me, eternal life: Never leave the knowledge of yourself. Then, put down as you are in the valley of humility, you will know me ...[23]

Being humbled by the truth of what we are is the beginning of being open to God, and his blessing of us. In the baptismal story which is the story of redemption, it is the cross of Christ – surrounded by betrayal, rejection, hatred – which shows up the truth about humanity. This cross stands as the ultimate place of honesty about human sin, and divine love. Here all that is good and loving is trampled underfoot; here too is the beginning of new, resurrected living. And from the cross itself Jesus speaks: 'Father, forgive them.'[24]

When this message is fully appropriated in our hearts and

minds, when it is lived in our lives, *then* we are, truly, 'free from sin'. Because here we encounter sin, as real-ly as ever, but not as the burden of guilt and pain, defensiveness and self-deceit – something we have to carry around with us forever, and find ways of covering up and excusing. No. Here, in the Christian life in Christ, sin is the place where we can turn in honesty and truth, and know God's love most fully for what it is: 'love to the loveless', that they might be lovely.[25]

It is at this point that we need to be reminded, again, that baptism is not a personal, me-and-God matter, but something which involves a whole people. In principle, baptism involves the whole of humanity, as it calls us to embody ever more deeply, in the world, the saving truth of redemption in Christ. We have seen that, when we acknowledge our sin, in the light and sureness of Christ's resurrection, we are freed from it through the knowledge of God's saving love. We are *forgiven*. But if we are, in this way, a people who live baptism as a sinning and forgiven people, we are also called to live baptism through the habitual and constant forgiving of others. If baptism makes us sharers in Christ's death, then we are surely, too, sharers in that move to forgive even those who crucify us.

Here is another crucial clue to the mystery of living as 'saved sinners' – the command to forgive.

FREE TO FORGIVE, FREE TO LOVE

There is something coming to light here, about sin and our liberation from it, which draws us close to the deepest mystery of all – God's love for us. What is clear is that freedom from sin is not the freedom to do whatever we want; nor is it, disappointingly, a freedom which means we don't need to be bothered by sin any more. What it *is* is that freedom, born of God's total forgiveness of us, to live our present and future in ways not structured around, and intractably shaped by past sin, mistakes, and wrongdoing. We are – *always and in principle* – free to start afresh. Sin – in our own lives and those of others – no longer needs to be what binds and shapes our emotions, relationships, possibilities and hopes; it remains a truly real part of our lives, but fails to be the abiding reality of who we are.

But the question remains: how come sin exists at all? This is a problem which has always troubled theologians and philosophers. If, after all, God created all things good, how can it be that we experience so much that is less than good, and is damaging and destructive?

St Augustine's somewhat startling conclusion to his deep and troubled thinking through of this question was that, in a real (though perhaps unusual) sense, evil and sin *didn't exist*! Evil is, in fact, no-thing at all.[26] Sin is nothing more (and nothing less) than the perversion of our human will, away from all that is good and true and beautiful in God and his creation, toward the dark unreality of our own version of things, our own desires, appetites, and self-importance. We imagine ourselves to be able to will things to be different from how God has made them, we live as if we were in fact in charge, creators ourselves. In this way we make the no-thing that is sin our most powerful reality.

Not everyone would find Augustine's account here satisfactory. For some it seems to weaken the real powerful presence of sin and evil in the world, as if the nothingness of evil meant we didn't need to worry about it any more. In fact, as Herbert McCabe points out, if you're driving towards the edge of the cliff, and the road is about to run out, it is *precisely* the nothing that you have to fear![27] For him, as for Augustine, the anti-reality which is the human perversion of life called sin, is desperately threatening, and death-dealing, for all that it is a lack, a no-thing. As the gaping hole of nothingness in God's good creation of everything, human sin has the power to deceive, deform, and enslave lives and whole cultures.

It is in this sense that we can begin to see in our baptismal living a freeing from sin. In baptism we are called, through Christ's death and resurrection, into the divine life of Trinity. *This* reality shows sin up for what it is: the threat and lostness of our own *nothings* as they fail, again and again, to speak the truth about what *is* real, and really *something* – God, and the life and love he holds toward us. Baptism, lived more and more deeply, has the power to free us from the tyrannical, self-constructed unreality which is sin, by drawing us closer to the reality which is life in Christ. And this is a life characterised by forgiveness: of my own sin, by God and others; and my forgiveness of the sins of others. A community that lived with this as its central reality of relationship would truly embody a living of baptism which was freeing of people, at the profoundest level of their being.

This forgiveness, and our frequent request for it in repentance, can remind us, again and again, of what is most real in baptised living: not who did what to who, and whose fault it is, and what should be done about it – but rather, that freedom to love and be loved in Christ, who has done all that needs to be done. It may not always feel like it, but *this* is the reality of Christian life. It is to this most real thing – God's love for us in all our muddle – that living baptism is called to witness.

LIVING THE MYSTERY

The theology of baptism discloses to us this odd truth: that we are to live as saved sinners, 'a chosen race, a royal priesthood, a holy nation, God's own people'.[28] This is where mystery becomes thoroughly mixed in with *ethic* – how we are actually to go about living, and doing the things we do.

This ethic, this way of holy living, is full of day-to-day challenges and graces. Living a life ordered to holiness, to God, in a world which is fallen and broken, and in which we know ourselves as sinful – well, this can feel like picking our way through a minefield, or navigating through dangerous reefs in stormy weather. We need to find guides, learn skills, and know the terrain better.

The Christian tradition is not without resources for such tutoring in holiness: the ten commandments, the many exhortations to holy living in the New Testament letters,[29] Jesus' own teaching in the Gospel accounts[30] – all these suggest that we are not without direction in coming to understand sin, and so knowing where to repent, and so how to be freed through God's forgiving love. The Christian tradition beyond the written testimony of Scripture has also sought to identify sin, as a help to our growth in repentance, forgiveness and holiness.[31] But for all this, we know that conversion of life can't, in the end, be simply a matter of keeping the rules – however important they, and obedience to them, might be. We cannot, after all, be holy *only* through an act of will on our own part. Somehow we need to learn something deeper: the reshaping of our own will and desires and appetites more closely in line with Christ and his call to us. And this reshaping, or configuring to Christ is, ultimately, the work of the Holy Spirit. What we can do is open the day-to-day fabric of our living and thinking and loving (and hating!) as much as we can to this work of God in us. This involves our efforts, and our taking on the rules set for us by our Christian tradition, to be sure: but it also requires the deeper transformation which is true repentance – *metanoia*, a turning around of life to God.

The following suggests a few ways in which this habit of repentance, and the choosing of the good in preference to the anti-reality of our own sin, might begin to grow in ordinary living.

SHAPING OUR THINKING THROUGH SCRIPTURE

As this chapter has shown, it is just about impossible to read the Gospel stories honestly, and avoid the question of sin, repentance and forgiveness. This language has always been there: what has sometimes been lacking is our attention to it, in the way we read, hear, or choose to interpret these texts. This is not surprising. For to read the Scriptures while being open to their message about sin makes a particular demand on us – that is, that we should allow ourselves to be convicted of our sins before these texts. It is, after all, those who know themselves as sinners who most readily hear God's word in Jesus' teaching, and the 'good' and upright Pharisees who have the problem. Our reading of Scripture needs to move us from devotion, or lofty thoughts, or improving reflection, into the painful reality of what we're really like. It's only in such an honest place that we can hear God's word for what it really is: the word of forgiveness, hope, love, and eternal life.

A prayer of repentance, or examination of conscience, can sometimes be a good place to begin our praying of the Bible texts. When we come to these readings full of anger, bitterness, resentment, or jealousy – well, we are hardly likely to encounter Christ, unless we first pray, 'Be merciful to me, a sinner.' From such a place of open reception to God's love we can hear with hope and strength his message of forgiveness and holy living, as it speaks from the Scriptures.

Stories of Jesus' compassion and power to forgive, to free us from, sin:

- Mark 1:1–5: this is how the 'good news of Jesus Christ' begins.
- Mark 2:1–12: the healing and forgiveness of the paralytic.

- Mark 2:15–17: Jesus spends time with sinners.
- Luke 6:27–36: learning to be merciful.
- Luke 7:36–50: the wholehearted repentance of the sinning woman, and her forgiveness.
- Luke 15:11–32: the prodigal son, and the extraordinary, unquestioning love of the father, who welcomes his return.
- Matthew 18:10–14: the lost sheep, whom God searches out, to rejoice over.
- John 8:2–11: Jesus' wisdom over the woman caught in adultery.

The presence of sin in the Christian's life, and the permanent call to repentance and struggle:

- Romans 7:14—8:2: Paul's own struggle with sin, and his freedom in Christ.
- 2 Corinthians 7:8–10: 'godly grief', repentance and peace through the argument of Christians.
- 1 John 1:5—2:2: self-deceit, the reality of sin, and the sureness of God's forgiveness of us in Christ.

The community of forgiveness:

- Matthew 5:43–8: the command to love our enemies.
- Matthew 18:21–2: Peter's question to Jesus about forgiving.
- 2 Corinthians 2:5–11: forgiving the offender, for his good, and the good of the community in fighting evil.

SIGNS AND SYMBOLS

The question of how our lives are furnished with signs and symbols that remind us of this great truth of sin and forgiveness is not an easy one. These things are, essentially, 'doings', rather than signs to ponder or contemplate. In the Catholic tradition we are most used to understanding sign and symbol through the language and celebration of sacraments: but, whilst we have a sacrament of confession or reconciliation,[32] it is comparatively lacking in concrete symbol and liturgical sign. Here is no water, no oil for anointing, no candles, no food and drink – simply the conversation, prayer, absolution and penance between penitent sinner and confessor. Perhaps it is the very 'bareness' of this celebration (for celebration it undoubtedly is!), which is its most eloquent sign, as we are stripped back to the basics of what we are before God. There is, after all, a time for an emptiness of symbol, a time for awful simplicity of self in the sight of God.

Yet the tradition is not without outward signs of penance and forgiveness. In Lent – the traditional time of repentance in preparation for Easter – the three great works of prayer, fasting and almsgiving are given central place. Here the disciplines of what we eat, of going without, and of giving to those in need, are proposed as effective ways of embodying our desire to repent. These are scriptural practices, well rooted in the long traditions of Christianity; they are, perhaps, things that need some place in the pattern of our contemporary lives as we struggle to live baptism. For some Christians each Friday is an opportunity to fast or limit what we eat in some way; for others the hard discipline of regular giving to those in need works to remind us of our need to learn unselfishness. Perhaps it is in a new approach to these 'acts of penance' – small, chosen ways of making our lives a little harder – that we can be reminded, in all our self-sufficiency and relative comfort, of our absolute dependence on the love of God. For sin, as we have seen, is above all the ignoring of God as our Creator, and the desire to do things our own way.[33] We need to enquire of our daily lives, where is my penance, my sorrow for sin, expressed?

FORMATION IN PRAYER

The model of Christian prayer given, the Scriptures tell us, by Jesus himself, is the Lord's Prayer; and it is striking that, in this prayer, we are called upon to ask forgiveness for our own sins, with the clear implication that we are commanded to forgive the sins of those who have hurt or damaged us. Prayers of sorrow and repentance, and prayers of love for our enemies are central to the prayer-life of the baptised person.

For many Christians, the liturgical celebration of the Eucharist begins with an expression of repentance; in its own way this is a recalling of that original repentance of baptism, and a confirmation that we do, indeed, desire a fresh start. At least sometimes, also, prayers of repentance are the place to begin our personal prayer. Certainly for myself, after a day of moans, and unkindness, and struggles with selfishness, getting back to God in prayer frequently needs to be through the genuine looking at the way I've behaved and being truly sorry for it. From such sorrow the request for God's forgiveness, enshrined in the Lord's Prayer, springs with heartfelt spontaneity; and, we can be sure, it is met with the immediate love of the Father, who runs out to meet the prodigal as she returns. This is, in the ordinary way of things, a frequently helpful beginning to time with God.

If there are, in prayer, times of clearly felt sorrow and repentance, there are, perhaps more frequently, times of simply feeling cut off from God, and not really knowing why. The wisdom of the spiritual tradition teaches us that the reasons for this may be many, and that, indeed, such feelings in prayer are not necessarily a bad thing. But there are times when this lostness in prayer is to do with our habits of sin, our almost unconscious drift into things less than what we are called to. In exploring this area of our fallenness, the tradition of praying an *examen* – an examination of conscience – is helpful. Responding to questions we pose ourselves as to how we live can disclose – gently but vividly – the truth about how our living does and doesn't measure up to life in Christ. The exact nature of those questions will vary; but however it is to happen, we need to find ways of asking how the various practices of our lives look in the light of our baptismal vocation. How I am a parent, how I am a colleague at work, or a spouse; how I use my money, my leisure time, gifts and talents; how far prayer, and faith, and talk about and with God figure in my day – all these are areas for examination, in the peaceful, secure knowledge that, in discovering more clearly the truth about the way we live, we will be enabled to know more fully the saving love of God for us.

The following is simply one example of how such an examination of conscience might look:

> Have I tried to love the Lord with my whole heart?
> Have I earnestly looked for him, in prayer and silence?
>
> Have I shown anger, or impatience, or lack of charity to anyone?
> Have I judged others harshly? Gossiped about them?
> Have I failed to forgive, or to seek forgiveness?
> Have I held on to resentments and hurts?

Have I done my work with honesty and integrity?
Have I witnessed to the Good News?
Have I relaxed and rested properly?
Or have I indulged wrongly in food, or drink?

Have I shown compassion to those in need?
Have I used my money, and my gifts for others and the Kingdom?
Have I worked to bring about God's justice?

LEARNING TO LOVE

Learning about sin and forgiveness is, in the end, learning in love. For those of us who live in households with other people, one of the most concrete signs which can help us on our way in this is a very human, relational thing. Living with others will always be the occasion of various kinds of sin! We are irritated, frustrated and in disagreement with our families; the constraints of living with others necessarily thwarts my selfish attempts to do simply what I want when I want – and this makes me crabby. Not only this, but the effort in keeping nice and polite and kind is pretty much unsustainable once we reach the place where we are at home, and relax into the tired, unguarded truth of what we're feeling. At home, with those closest to us, irritability and unkindness abound.

All this seems to me pretty much inevitable, human beings being what they are. The question is, how to respond, as people called to live baptism, to these ordinary realities. And perhaps the suggestion I want to give sounds too simple, too obvious, to be helpful: we should, *habitually*, say 'sorry' to those around us when these moments strike; and we should learn the habit, too, of letting go of the hurt that others do to us, in the ordinary run of things.

If these are obvious, uncontroversial things to say, they are, none the less, rather difficult to do. It is easier, especially in households, to *assume* we are forgiven, understood, and that things will blow over; often if we just move on from that hurt we did to our friend, or the hurt they did us, we can, seemingly, get back on track. But maybe such 'getting on with it' also lets us all off the hook, lets us go on pretending that, actually, it's OK for me to be hurtful or careless of another's feelings, or that it isn't really my fault because I was tired, or stressed. There is a real effort involved in saying 'sorry' for the little thing – the snapped reply, the ratty mood, the lack of warmth and welcome. But what this chapter has to say about the Gospel tradition of sin and forgiveness suggests, to me, that there is a real way through to joy and growth in these apparently small moments of reconciliation. It is here that we learn to love, and to know ourselves as loved.

The chances are, if we were to examine our consciences each night before we sleep, we would find, most days, more than one person to whom we might say sorry; there is also likely to be hurt, which calls us to forgive somebody else – though my own experience is that I have to pray pretty hard for the grace to be able to do this! Even my own act of forgiving depends on the Lord!

To develop such a habit of sorrow and forgiveness is a remarkable tutoring in Christian love. In this learning each morning could break as a genuinely fresh start, for us, and for those with whom we come into contact. We might, in this way, begin to build patterns of human living, in Christ, more and more deeply freed from sin. This would be living baptism indeed.

EPILOGUE

LIVING BAPTISM: MISSION AND MYSTERY

Imprisoned in Nazi Germany in May 1944, less than a year before his execution, the great Lutheran pastor and theologian Dietrich Bonhoeffer wrote to his infant great-nephew on the occasion of his baptism.[1] It is a profoundly moving letter, which draws together the great troubles of that time, with the happier times of Bonhoeffer's own childhood, and from the hopelessness of the prison cell, finds a voice for hope and the future. At the end of our exploration of baptism and its liveliness for the third millennium, it is remarkable to read this witness of 60 years ago and recognise its concerns.

Bonhoeffer, in all his mature works, is properly preoccupied with what it can mean, in practice, to be the Church, the Christian community, in a Europe which seemed increasingly Godless. He recognised, with extraordinary insight, not only the evils of his own time and place, but the great shifts in thinking and life that must follow on from the tragedies of the first half of the twentieth century: the radical secularisation of society, the effects of fear and the knowledge of humanity's own potential for self-destruction, the profound failure of the organisational churches in resisting evils in the world – Bonhoeffer instinctively saw all this on the horizon. This insight led him not to despair, but to a quiet, strange kind of hope. Specifically, it was his faith that the future belonged to God, and that as long as a few prayed and lived the Gospel, even as a 'secret discipline',[2] then we had every reason to hope that the world would be renewed.

There are some compelling connections between this letter from a previous time and our own concerns. Indeed, the connection jumps out to meet us in the opening paragraph, which speaks into the future of the baptised infant, and refers to the time of his maturity 'long after the year 2000'.[3] Bonhoeffer's deep sense of connection in addressing this new Christian, this first of a new generation, enables him to address the start of the new millennium – our own time. This is a time, he suggests, when the most pressing concern of the Christian disciple must be how to speak to ordinary 'religionless' or secular men and women – like us. The celebration of baptism which he contemplates is a reminder both of the eternal truths of our redemption, and of the apparently insurmountable difficulties we face in understanding and communicating them today. So he writes:

> Reconciliation and redemption, regeneration and the Holy Spirit, love of our enemies, cross and resurrection, life in Christ and Christian discipleship – all these things are so difficult and so remote that we hardly venture any more to speak of them. In the traditional words and acts we suspect that there may be something quite new and revolutionary, though we cannot as yet grasp or express it. That is our own fault. Our church, which has been fighting in these years only for its own self-preservation, as though that were an end in itself, is incapable of taking the word of reconciliation and redemption to mankind and the world.[4]

This account of things, even at over 60 years' distance, and written in quite a different set of circumstances from our own, still has some very clear resonance with where we find ourselves today. In our radically secular, post-modern and post-Christian societies, the freshness and permanently contemporary vitality of Christian living all too often seems lost for words, whilst the church organisations frequently seem more intent on maintenance of their own structures, than on the building of hope and joy and fullness of life in the ordinary misery and burden of human lives. Bonhoeffer's reading of the condition of modern Christianity is not so very different from that of this book.[5] Also similar is his hint at how things are to proceed from such an apparently lost and difficult place.

Dietrich Bonhoeffer's departing prayer for his great-nephew, at his baptism, is that he should be one of those faithful disciples who, through all the coming difficulties and lostness of 'religion', remain in prayer, waiting on the Lord. We can be certain, Bonhoeffer writes, that, in God's own time, human living of the Gospel will be renewed: 'Till then the Christian cause will be a silent and hidden affair, but there will be those who pray and do right and wait for God's own time.'[6] Indeed, it is precisely from this hidden, quiet place of faithfulness, prayer, and living goodness, in the ordinary 'secular' lives of men and women – from *here* 'all Christian thinking, speaking and organising must be born anew'.[7] This living of baptismal discipleship is the basis of hope for the future of humanity: and it is, believes Bonhoeffer, a sure ground for hope.

These reflections not only echo, in brief, what the words of this book have tried to express in more detail; they also encapsulate one crucial, final theme for us: what we might most simply call 'the future'. For above all, Bonhoeffer's meditations from his prison cell, on baptism and family and domestic life, refer us to *time*. Specifically, we are drawn into an interweaving of past, present and future, which refers us to *God's own time*. This is a time which always lies ahead of us – *future*.

By letting baptism refer us to the time ahead, in a way deeply informed by past traditions, and the living of present faith, we are drawn into the future in a particular way. We are called out from here – into our next minute, day, decade – in a manner which describes that future time both as mystery and as mission. If we are to let the life of Christ grow, not through our planning, but through our daily openness to God, we will become more and more aware how mysterious is this Trinitarian life. This future is not something to be managed, or aimed at; rather it is to be received, in prayer and holy living, and the steady, patient, waiting on God in the ordinariness of life. The mystery of the extraordinary truth that God is with us, leading us on, can only become real through such painstaking attentiveness.

In this ever-coming mystery of the future we will meet, too, with all the occasions for mission – for communication of the Gospel and the joy of its living – that we could wish for; far more than we could ever engineer or organise for ourselves! The living of baptism, which this book has tried to describe, is characterised by opening the everyday and ordinary to the profound mystery of life in Christ. When this takes place, even in some small way, our present is transformed by openness to God's future; and in *this* place the mission of the Gospel becomes a living power to save, make joyful, transform, and make more fully human. Living baptism means ever looking to the next moment, and knowing it as a moment graced by mystery and by mission.

In this way we are left, in the end, at the place where we started, but seeing it rather differently. Just as baptism begins the Gospel narratives, so, too, in Matthew's Gospel, does it close the story; but here baptism is not an event, but a call to the next thing. Jesus has risen from the dead, and met with his disciples. His last encounter with them, according to this Gospel, goes like this:

> Jesus came and said to them, 'All authority in heaven and on earth has been given to me. Go, therefore, and make disciples of all the nations, baptising them in the name of the Father, and of the Son, and of the Holy Spirit, and teaching them to obey everything that I have commanded you. And remember, I am with you always, to the end of the age.'[8]

In the end, this is where living baptism brings us: to the place of being sent out, by the risen Jesus, to do the work which, for each of us, lies ahead. It is a work intimately bound up with baptism itself, and with attentiveness to the Lord's teaching. More than that, it is a way ahead in which we are called, always, to *remember* that God is with us – to the end.

The next step, the next bit of the future: this is where the living of baptism begins – always.

NOTES

1. BAPTISM AND CHRISTIAN DISCIPLESHIP

1. A substantial and profound reflection on this is to be found in A. Schmemann, *By Water and the Spirit: A Liturgical Study of Baptism* (St Vladimir's Seminary Press, New York, 1995). In this book the Orthodox rite of baptism is explained and explored as a way of drawing out the profound theology of Christian life which it proclaims. It is a book to which the present author is indebted.
2. Formula from the *Roman Rites* of baptism. See, too, the signing of the cross in the baptismal rites of *Common Worship.*
3. See Chapter 5 below.
4. So see the World Council of Churches' document, *Baptism, Eucharist and Ministry* (Faith & Order Paper 111, 1982) on baptism, n. 20. This normative insistence on water as the sacramental sign shouldn't, however, make us forgetful of the traditional reading of martyrdom for Christ (even of the unbaptised) as a baptism by blood, nor the significant Roman Catholic teaching on baptism by desire. *Catechism of the Catholic Church,* 1258–9.
5. More about this is said in Chapters 5 and 6 below.
6. *Catechism of the Catholic Church,* 1243. A tradition going back to ancient times, and connected with the Pauline idea that, in baptism, we are 'clothed with Christ' (Gal. 3:27).
7. E.g. *Common Worship* rites of baptism.
8. Tertullian, *On Baptism* 2. Translation from *The Ante-Nicene Fathers* (T. & T. Clark, reprint 1997), vol. III, p. 669.
9. From the ancient Easter hymn, 'The Exultet', solemnly sung as the first proclamation of Easter at the Easter Vigil in the New Roman Rite: 'Night truly blessed, when heaven is wedded to earth, and man is reconciled to God!'

2. BAPTISM AND THE RESHAPING OF 'CHURCH'

1. For example, World Council of Churches' *Baptism, Eucharist and Ministry* (Faith & Order Paper 111, 1982), Baptism 6; *Catechism of the Catholic Church* 1267–70.
2. A false dichotomy, in many ways – as this chapter, and, indeed, this book sets out to show. But, none the less, this is a distinction recognisable in the Christian tradition: 'If you belonged to the world, the world would love you as its own. Because you do not belong to the world, but I have chosen you out of the world – therefore the world hates you' (Jesus' words to his disciples in John 15:19).

3. I am thinking especially of Leonardo Boff, *Ecclesiogenesis: Base communities reinvent the church* (1986); and L. Segundo, *The Sacraments Today* (Gill & Macmillan, 1980).
4. See Luke 10:38–42.
5. Enda McDonagh, 'Fruit of the earth – work of human hands: a prophetic theology of the Eucharist', in M. Grey, A. Heaton & D. Sullivan (eds), *The Candles are still Burning: Directions in Sacrament and Spirituality* (Geoffrey Chapman, London, 1995), pp. 22–3.
6. A useful and more accessible account than many of our contemporary Western culture can be found in *On the Way to Life*, commissioned and published by the Catholic Education Service (CES) of the Bishops' Conference of England and Wales, 2005.
7. 'The man of today seems ever to be under threat from what he produces, that is to say from the result of the work of his hands and, even more so, of the work of his intellect and the tendencies of his will ... Man therefore lives increasingly in fear ... he is afraid that it [his work] can become the means and instrument for an unimaginable self-destruction, compared with which all the cataclysms and catastrophes of history known to us seem to fade away' (John Paul II, *Redemptor hominis* 15).
8. John Paul II, *Fides et Ratio* 6.
9. A reference, again, to the story of Mary and Martha, where Martha is judged by Jesus as fussing over things that are not needful: in fact, Jesus tells her, 'there is need of only one thing' (Luke 10:42).
10. The Toronto Statement, *Walk in Newness of Life*, Findings of the Fourth International Anglican Liturgical Consultation, Toronto 1991 (Grove Worship Series no. 118).
11. The image drawn fundamentally from 1 Cor. 12. More is said of this in Chapter 7 below.
12. Vatican II's Dogmatic Constitution on the Church, *Lumen Gentium*, ch. 1.
13. A term used by Romano Guardini.
14. *Lumen Gentium* 39–41.
15. Eph. 2:19–22.
16. There will be much more to say about this later, especially in Chapter 7.
17. Augustine, Sermon 46. Quoted from its use in the Roman *Office of Readings* for the 24th Sunday of the year.
18. John 15:18ff.

3. THE TRADITION OF BAPTISM AS VOCATION

1. I am indebted here to the helpful essay of Rowan Williams, where he discusses sacraments as rites of 'dislocation', rather than the more habilitating, comforting 'rites of passage'. Rowan Williams, 'Sacraments of the New Society' in D. Brown & A. Loades (eds), *Christ: the sacramental Word* (1996).

2. *Baptism, Eucharist and Ministry* (WCC Faith & Order Paper 111, 1982), Ref. 'Baptism', art. 2.
3. For example, at the end of Peter's speech at Pentecost (Acts 2:38ff); the conversion of Simon Magus and his followers on hearing Philip preach (Acts 8:9ff); the faith of the Ethiopian eunuch (Acts 8:35ff); et al.
4. E.g., Mark 1:4.
5. Mark 1:9–11; Matt. 3:16–17; Luke 3:21–2; John 1:32ff.
6. So see Mark 1:12; Matt. 4:1.
7. Luke 12:49–50.
8. Mark 10:38. See Mark 10:35–45 and Matt. 20:20–28.
9. Luke 3:22; Mark 1:11; Matt. 3:17.
10. Matt. 3:11.
11. Acts 2:37–42.
12. Acts 10:44–8.
13. Acts 16:15.
14. Acts 8:13.
15. 1 Cor. 1:10–17.
16. 1 Cor. 12:13.
17. Gal. 3:27.
18. 1 Cor. 1:10ff.
19. 1 Cor. 1:14–17.
20. Rom. 6:1–4.
21. That is, language of a more philosophical kind, which speaks about the nature of our very being.
22. *Catechism of the Catholic Church* (Geoffrey Chapman, 1994), para. 1280.
23. See Thomas Aquinas, *Summa Theologiae* III, 63.
24. See Gal. 3:27—4:7.
25. It should be clear from this section why it is that all the mainstream Christian communities reject, in accordance with the earliest Church, the practice of 're-baptism'.
26. *Catechism of the Catholic Church*, op. cit., 1272.
27. See J. F. White, *The Sacraments in Protestant Practice and Faith* (Nashville, 1999), p. 34, where he cites Luther's own treatise, 'The Holy and Blessed Sacrament of Baptism', in *Luther's Works*, vol. 35.
28. Ibid.
29. John Calvin, *Institutes of the Christian Religion*, book IV, ch. 15, art. 3.
30. Second Vatican Council's Dogmatic Constitution on the Church, *Lumen Gentium*, ch. II, 'The People of God'.
31. *Lumen Gentium* 10–11.
32. Ibid., 12.
33. Ibid., 13.
34. *Walk in Newness of Life. The findings of the fourth international Anglican*

liturgical consultation, Toronto 1991 (Grove Books, Grove Worship Series No. 118).

35. J. F. White, op. cit., p. 71.
36. Eph. 1:9–10.
37. K. Rahner, *Meditations on the Sacraments* (Burns & Oates, 1977), p. 15.
38. A. Schmemann, *Of Water and the Spirit. A Liturgical Study of Baptism* (St Vladimir's Seminary Press, 1974), p. 8.
39. Ibid., p. 9.

4. 'IN THE NAME OF THE FATHER, AND OF THE SON, AND OF THE HOLY SPIRIT'

1. So see, from earliest times, the *Didache* and early rites in E. C. Whitaker, *Documents of the Baptismal Liturgy* (SPCK, 1997). And in contemporary rites; see, e.g., Roman Rites of Christian Initiation; *Common Worship: Initiation Services*; et al.
2. Luke 1:35.
3. E.g. Matt. 11:25; Mark 14:36; John 17:1.
4. E.g. Luke 3:22; Mark 9:7.
5. John 16:5–15.
6. Rom. 8:15–17.
7. Heb. 12:22–3.
8. Mark 1:9–12.
9. This sense of the oddness of Jesus' baptism is hinted at in the story itself, as told in Matt. 3:13ff, where John is reluctant to baptise the Lord.
10. For a systematic account of the deliberations over the person of Christ at the Councils of Nicea (AD 325) and Chalcedon (AD 451), and their culmination in the doctrinal spelling out of the doctrine of the Trinity, see W. Kasper, *The God of Jesus Christ* (SCM, 1983), pp. 233–61; J. N. D. Kelly, *Early Christian Doctrines* (5th edn, A. & C. Black, 1977), pp. 109ff, 252ff.
11. Catherine Pickstock, *After Writing. The Liturgical Consummation of Philosophy* (Blackwell, 1997), pp. 181f.
12. So see Catherine Mowry La Cugna, *God for Us* (HarperSanFrancisco, 1991).
13. Cf. Matt. 17:5.
14. Catherine Pickstock, op. cit., p. 182.
15. F. Schleiermacher, *The Christian Faith*, ed. H. R. Mackintosh & J. S. Stewart (T. & T. Clark, 1999). The final sections of this work of Christian theology make clear Schleiermacher's concern for a more immediately meaningful understanding of the nature of God.
16. It is, perhaps, Karl Barth's work, which self-consciously rejects the position of Schleiermacher and those who developed his thought, that is most important here. So see his *Church Dogmatics* I/1, paras. 8–9.

17. Gregory Nazianzen, Basil and Gregory of Nyssa. See J. N. D. Kelly, *Early Christian Doctrines*, op. cit., pp. 263ff.
18. This 'savage' theological approach to language is beautifully articulated by H. McCabe in *God Matters* (Geoffrey Chapman, 1987), in McCabe's debate with 'G. Egner' on Eucharist and language, chs. 10–14.
19. John 3:16.
20. Rom. 8:15f.
21. *Quasi ignoto*, so see, e.g., *Summa Theologiae* 1a, 12.
22. *Pseudo-Dionysius: the complete works* (Classics of Western Spirituality, Paulist Press, 1987), p. 135.
23. Gal. 2:20.
24. 1 John 4:18.
25. This is the response of Mary, Mother of Jesus, when faced with the joyful and troubling mysteries of the Lord's life – Luke 2:19, 51.
26. One of the most outstanding examples of this would be found in the writings of St John of the Cross (16th century). See the collection of his works published in the Classics of Western Spirituality series (Paulist Press).

5. BAPTISM AS THE TOMB: SHARING IN CHRIST'S DEATH

1. Gal. 2:19–20.
2. Luke 7:50.
3. W. Pannenberg in D. Brown & A. Loades (eds), *Christ: the sacramental Word* (1996), p. 83.
4. 1 Cor. 2:2.
5. 1 Cor. 1:18–25.
6. For a study of St Mark's Gospel see, e.g., C. E. B. Cranfield, *The Gospel according to St Mark. An introduction and commentary* (Cambridge University Press, 1983).
7. So see Jesus in Gethsemane, Mark 14:32–6.
8. Judas' kiss, Mark 14:43–5.
9. In Gethsemane and Peter's later denials – Mark 14:37–42, 66–72.
10. Mark 8:27–31.
11. Mark 8:34.
12. Matt. 10, esp. vv. 37–9; Luke 14:25–33.
13. John 15:12–17.
14. John 21:15–19.
15. Col. 1:20.
16. Rom. 5:8–9.
17. Col. 2:14–15.
18. E.g. as implied in Gal. 3:13.
19. This is the argument of 1 Pet. 2:13ff.

20. For some account of these 'models' of atonement, see S. W. Sykes, *The Story of Atonement* (Darton, Longman & Todd, 1997), esp. pp. 1–36.
21. H. McCabe, *God Still Matters* (Continuum, 2002), p. 96.
22. Ibid., p. 97.
23. 1 Cor. 1.
24. Jesus' cry from the cross as he dies, according to Matt. 27:46.
25. Apostolic Letter, *Salvifici Doloris*, 1984.
26. These are well documented in *St Therese of Lisieux: her last conversations* (trans. John Clarke, Institute of Carmelite Studies, 1977).
27. Rom. 6:4.
28. E.g. Ignatius' *Letter to the Ephesians* 18; *Letter to the Magnesians* 5. These can be found in *Early Christian Writings*, trans. M. Staniforth (Penguin Classics, 1980).
29. Ibid., *Letter to the Romans* 2.
30. Ibid., 4.
31. Ibid., 6.
32. Ibid.
33. Ibid., 7.
34. St Jane Frances de Chantal (1572–1641), *Memoirs* III, 3 (1853). Taken from the *Divine Office*, office of readings for the feast of St Jane Frances de Chantal, 12 December.
35. Ibid.
36. Gal. 2:20.
37. Eph. 3:20.
38. John 3:16.
39. Quoted in *The SPCK Book of Christian Prayer* (SPCK, 1999), p. 398.

6. BAPTISM AS THE WOMB: SHARING IN CHRIST'S RESURRECTION

1. Rom. 6:4–5.
2. See E. C. Whitaker, *Documents of the Baptismal Liturgy* (SPCK, 1970), p. 2.
3. *Apostolic Tradition of Hippolytus* xxii. See E. C. Whitaker, op. cit., p. 6.
4. See, e.g., the instruction set out in *The Rites of the Catholic Church, vol. I* (Liturgical Press, 1990), pp. 37–8.
5. John 3:1–8.
6. *Common Worship: Initiation Services* (Church House, 1998), p. 19.
7. E.g., H. J. Richards, *The First Easter: what really happened?* (Collins, 1976).
8. Appointed in 1984, amid some controversy regarding his comments on resurrection.
9. H. McCabe, *God Still Matters* (Continuum, 2002), p. 227.
10. Mark 16:6.
11. So see Luke 24:1–12; Matt. 28:1–10.
12. John 20:1–18.

13. Luke 24:13–35.
14. John 21:4–14.
15. John 20:24–9.
16. Acts 1:6–11.
17. Acts 1:6.
18. Acts 1:12–14.
19. Rom. 8:9–11.
20. 1 Cor. 12:13.
21. Eph. 4:5.
22. Matt. 10:34.
23. W. Pannenberg, 'Baptism as remembered "ecstatic" identity', in D. Brown & A. Loades (eds), *Christ: The Sacramental Word* (1996), p. 85.
24. Col. 3:1–4.
25. John 3:8.
26. It seems clear to me that what the Montanist prophetesses actually taught was hardly heretical, though sometimes a bit odd or extreme. For an account of this schism see, e.g., W. H. C. Frend, *The Early Church. From the beginnings to 461* (SCM, 1982), pp. 69ff.
27. Rom. 8:18.
28. Rom. 8:15–16.
29. John 14:23.

7. SHARING IN CHRIST'S BODY: A COMMUNION OF SAINTS

1. *The Rites of the Catholic Church, vol. I* (Liturgical Press, 1990), p. 217.
2. Ibid., p. 378.
3. Karl Rahner, *Meditations on the Sacraments* (Burns & Oates, 1977), pp. 13–14.
4. 1 Cor. 12:12–13.
5. John Calvin, *Institutes of the Christian Religion*, book iv, ch. 15.
6. Vatican II Dogmatic Constitution on the Church, *Lumen Gentium* 7.
7. Gal. 3:27–8.
8. Eph. 4:4–6.
9. Quoted from the 1552 Anglican rite of baptism in J. F. White, *The Sacraments in Protestant Practice and Faith* (1999), p. 46.
10. So see the Roman Catholic *Rite of Christian Initiation of Adults*; the Anglican Communion's statement on baptism, *Walk in Newness of Life*, Findings of the Fourth International Anglican Liturgical Consultation, Toronto 1991 (Grove Worship Series no. 118); the World Council of Churches' statement on baptism in *Baptism, Eucharist and Ministry* (Faith & Order Paper 111, 1982); et al.
11. I am indebted to my colleague, Dr Susan Parsons, for this type of phrase in the passive voice. This perhaps difficult or odd-sounding language none the less expresses well a proper 'passivity' in relation

to Church and discipleship. For the disciple, both Church and life are focused on God's activity, not our own.

12. See esp. 1 Cor. 12—13.
13. John 15:1–11.
14. For the background to 1 Corinthians see J. C. Hurd, *The origins of I Corinthians* (SPCK, 1965).
15. See Eph. 4:15–16; Col. 1:18.
16. J. Moltmann, *The Church in the Power of the Spirit* (SCM Press, 1977), pp. 68–75.
17. Some account of this is given in the short, scholarly book by Nicholas Sagovsky, *Ecumenism, Christian Origins, and the Practice of Communion* (Cambridge University Press, 2000). For a general overview, see pp. 18–47.
18. So see *ARCIC, The Final Report* (CTS/SPCK, 1982).
19. *The Nature & Purpose of the Church* (Faith & Order Paper No. 181).
20. Especially John Zizioulas, *Being as Communion. Studies in Personhood and the Church* (St Vladimir Seminary Press, 1993).
21. *The Nature & Purpose of the Church*, op. cit. The document follows the WCC convention of keeping the main body of the text for describing what is agreed upon by the different Christian communities, whilst attesting to areas of disagreement through the marginal texts, framed by boxes.
22. Matt. 6:6.
23. Interestingly, Jonathan Robinson (Cong. Orat.) links this contemporary emphasis in the Church to the influence of philosophical and cultural changes since the Enlightenment. Whilst, in the end, I find myself in some serious disagreement with his book, his study of modernity and its possible influence on Catholic self-understanding is provocative and clear: *The Mass and Modernity. Walking to Heaven Backward* (Ignatius Press, 2005).
24. The 'Preliminary Explanatory Note' appended to the Council's Dogmatic Constitution on the Church, *Lumen Gentium.*
25. As in Denys the Areopagite's *Ecclesiastical Hierarchies* of the sixth century.
26. Paul McPartlan's study of Henri de Lubac and John Zizioulas has renewed our sense of the 'Eucharist making Church', in correction to an over-emphasis on 'Church making Eucharist'. So see P. McPartlan, *The Eucharist makes the church. Henri de Lubac and John Zizioulas in dialogue* (T. & T. Clark, 1993); or, more accessibly, his *Sacrament of Salvation. An introduction to Eucharistic Ecclesiology* (T. & T. Clark, 1995).
27. Augustine, Sermon 272, as quoted (my addition in square brackets) in *Catechism of the Catholic Church* 1396.
28. Congregation for the Doctrine of the Faith (CDF), *Letter on Aspects of the Church considered as Communion* (1992), article 4.

29. Nicholas Lash, *His Presence in the World. A study in eucharistic worship and theology* (Sheed & Ward, 1968; 4th impression 1980). The argument of ch. 5 explicates this idea well.
30. As Justin Martyr describes in the second century. So see H. Bettenson (ed.), *Documents of the Christian Church* (Oxford University Press, 1963), p. 66.
31. This is well described by the Second Vatican Council's Dogmatic Constitution on Divine Revelation, *Dei Verbum*, esp. art. 11.
32. *Dei Verbum*, op. cit., art. 8.
33. 1 Cor. 12:26.
34. Matt. 5:44.
35. For some history of the term, and a critical account of it see J. C. Atkinson, 'Family as Domestic Church. Developmental trajectory, legitimacy, and problems of appropriation', in *Theological Studies* 66, no. 3 (Sept. 2005); and Clare Watkins, '*Traditio* – the Ordinary Handling of Holy Things', in *New Blackfriars* vol. 87 (March 2006), pp. 164ff.

8. 'WASHED CLEAN'? LIVING AS SAVED SINNERS

1. 1 Pet. 2:9.
2. E.g., *Common Worship: Initiation Services* (Church House, 1998), p. 22.
3. Mark 1:4.
4. Mark 1:1.
5. *Catechism of the Catholic Church* (Geoffrey Chapman, 1994), para. 1263.
6. Vatican II Pastoral Constitution on the Church in the Modern World, *Gaudium et Spes*, ch. I.
7. Mark 1:4.
8. Luke 1:77.
9. Mark 1:15; Matt. 4:17.
10. Mark 2:5ff; Luke 7:36ff.
11. Mark 2:15–17.
12. Ibid.; Luke 19:9–10.
13. Matt. 26:27–8.
14. Gen. 1—3.
15. Gen. 1:26–7.
16. *Catechism of the Catholic Church*, op. cit., 404–5, where 'original sin' is described as a 'state' rather than a personal act.
17. For some account of this see J. Martos, *Doors to the Sacred* (Doubleday, 1982), pp. 315ff.
18. As referenced by J. N. D. Kelly, *Early Christian Doctrines* (5th edn, A. & C. Black, 1980), p. 413.
19. Ibid., p. 416. A helpful lengthy excerpt from Augustine's *On Baptism* discussing this theme can be easily found in M. Wiles & M. Santer, *Documents in Early Christian Thought* (Cambridge University Press, 1979), pp. 163–6.

20. Luke 18:9–14.
21. Luke 7:47–8.
22. Easily accessible in the edition published by Penguin Classics, translated by R. S. Pine-Coffin.
23. Catherine of Siena, *The Dialogue* (Classics of Western Spirituality, Paulist Press, 1980), p. 29.
24. Luke 23:34.
25. Taken from that great Passiontide hymn, 'My song is love unknown', written by Samuel Crossman (1624–83).
26. One of the best, and most readable accounts of this is given by Herbert McCabe in *God Matters* (Geoffrey Chapman, 1987), ch. 3, 'Evil'. The same tradition is also witnessed to in a sensitively personal way by Simon Tugwell, *Prayer, vol 1. Living with God* (Veritas, Dublin, 1974), esp. ch. 3.
27. Herbert McCabe, *God Matters*, op. cit., p. 29.
28. 1 Pet. 2:9.
29. E.g. Rom. 12:9–21; Gal. 6:1–10; Eph. 4:25—5:20; et al.
30. Probably the most notable – though not the only – example of this would be the great section of teaching in the Sermon on the Mount, esp. Matt. 5:21—7:23.
31. So the various catechisms, examinations of conscience etc. produced through the Christian generations, as an aid to identifying sin in the muddle of Christian living.
32. Interestingly, the first name given to this sacrament in the *Catechism of the Catholic Church* is the sacrament of *conversion*, op. cit., 1423.
33. Simon Tugwell's account of the fall and sin is very helpful in illuminating this. *Prayer, vol. 1*, op. cit., pp. 31–44.

EPILOGUE

1. Dietrich Bonhoeffer, *Letters and Papers from Prison* (SCM, 1971), pp. 294ff. I am grateful to Fr David Hennessey, parish priest, who, in the weeks in which I struggled to complete this book, reminded me of this text.
2. A phrase especially characteristic of his last writings. See *Letters and Papers*, op. cit., pp. 280–82, 286, et al.
3. Ibid., p. 294.
4. Ibid., pp. 299–300.
5. So see Chapter 2 above.
6. *Letters and Papers*, op. cit., p. 300.
7. Ibid.
8. Matt. 28:18–20.

REFERENCES FROM THE NEW TESTAMENT

GENERAL INDEX